The
LIGHT
in the
MIDST
of
DARKNESS

GENEVA LOFTON

Auctorem House
276 5th Ave, Ste 704-2591
New York, NY 10001
www.auctoremhouse.com
1.888.332.7718

CONTENTS

ACKNOWLEDGEMENTS

I would like to acknowledge my Lord and Savior Jesus Christ for sparing my life from so many close to death experiences that I've had. I thank Him for being my Savior and my Lord. I acknowledge my son, Timothy and my grandson, Tyrran, for loving me unconditionally. I acknowledge my pastors, the late Kenneth Lee Lofton and Co-Pastor Helen Lofton that preached the gospel in truth, love, and with authority; for they truly have encouraged me whenever I needed it the most. They have always prayed for me and they have pointed me into the direction of God's love and His word.

DEDICATION

I would like to dedicate this book first of all to God the Father, the Son, and the Holy Spirit. Also, this book is dedicated to my son and grandson, Timothy Jerome Manning Jr. and Tyrran Jashaun Manning. Finally, I dedicate this book in loving memory of my mom and dad, the late Willie James Lofton and the late Tenie Mae Barnes Lofton.

INTRODUCTION

I wanted to write a book to inspire everyone to follow his or her dreams and destiny in Christ Jesus. Many times society counts people out, but God has a purpose for each and every person that has ever been born and that will ever be born. We are not an afterthought. God loves all of us, but He hates sin. No matter what situations in our lives may arise, good or not so good, Jesus loves us. He always wants the best for those that love Him and that will give their lives to Him so that He can use them for His glory.

Watch out for individuals that are sent into your life to manipulate, distract, and cause you to lose your soul to an eternal darkness and damnation. Ask God for a spirit of discernment so that the enemy will not continue to make a fool out of you. Guard your heart and please don't despise wisdom and constructive criticism that can save you a lot of heartache, headache and pain in the long run.

Those wrong choices that I have made in life, I had to forgive myself and I continue to forgive others, but I don't want to continue to be a footstool and naïve. I put my trust in God because I know that He knows the past, present, and the future. If I seek God for directions and be obedient to the word of God, I will have some testing, trials, and tribulations. Yet, I know that in the midst of the darkness, God will forever be my eternal light.

ONE

My Childhood and My Family

HI, MY NAME is Geneva Lofton. I am 55 years old. I was born on August 16, 1969. I was born and raised in Lucama, North Carolina. I am the 10th and last child that my mom had. Yet, dad had 15 plus children in all. Yet, my brother, Kenneth, told me that whenever I was born that I used to sleep in a drawer in the dresser. Ummmmmm, I wonder if that's the reason why my head is flat in the back, and my butt is kind of flat too. Well, it's too late. I can't help the way God has made me. I need to be proud of who I am and know that I am beautiful.

I have a son and a grandson. My son's name is Timothy Jerome Manning Jr., and my grandson's name is Tyrran Jashaun Manning. We lived in the projects on Forrest Road, but the project mentality is not in us. I know that a lot of people say bad things about project housing, but I minded my own business, and I allowed God to help me strive for stability for my son, grandson, and myself.

Growing up was a lot of fun and surprises for myself and my siblings. We ate food that children would turn their noses up at in the time that we live in today. Since my dad was half-Indian and a hunter, we ate animals that my dad would hunt and kill like: rabbits, birds and etc. We ate the homemade biscuits and good food that my mom prepared for us every day. She was a cooking woman, and plenty of people have set up under her table and bragged about how good she used to cook.

We worked in tobacco, the cucumber fields, and in the gardens. Working together with your family really is very exciting. Even though I used to get really dirty while working in tobacco, picking cucumbers, and working in the garden, it was worthwhile. I believe that being able to work early in life made me feel like I had contributed to the family business.

We had our family time with each other, and we also had great fun whenever we invited relatives, friends, and workers to join in with us at our kitchen table. In the summer time for lunch, my siblings and I would get a quilt and lay on the wood floor. Then we would turn on the fan and go to sleep. That cool breeze upon my head would make me so relaxed. Then of course, it was time to get back to work after lunch and go back to putting in tobacco.

My mother is the late Tenie Mae Barnes Lofton and my father is the late Willies James Lofton. I am the tenth child that my mom birthed. My brother that was born before me is up in heaven. He died in my mother's womb. I have six sisters and their names are Carolyn Lofton Taylor, Carolyn Lofton Crumel, Christine Crumel, Frostina Renfrow, Lisa Tucker, and Sequania Edwards. I had 8 brothers, but unfortunately 3 brothers passed away. Their names are Frank James Lofton, the late Jesse James Lofton, Johnie Ray Lofton, Rudolph Lofton, the late Kenneth Lee Lofton, Kenneth Ray Tucker, the late baby boy Lofton, and Frederick Tyrone Lofton. All of us but four have the same mother and father, but it doesn't matter.

I let the pass be in the past. I love all of my siblings just as if we had the same parents.

My grandfather on my mom's side of the family was the late Rossie Lee Barnes, and my grandmother was the late Mamie Roundtree Barnes. I believe that my great grandmother on my mom's side of the family was the late Becky Pate. Our family cemetery in Lucama, North Carolina is called "The Becky Pate Cemetery" also known as "The Barnes Cemetery". It is named after my great grandmother.

I don't know a lot of people on my father's side of the family. My dad's mother was the late Rosa Lofton from Seven Springs or Indian Springs, North Carolina. I had met my aunt, the late Frances Gordon who died in 2009. I had met my uncle, the late Jesse James Lofton for the first time at my aunt's funeral. For the last couple of years, I had been going to the Lofton/Loftin Family Reunion so that I could get familiar with some of the dad's relatives.

My mom, the late Tenie Mae Barnes Lofton was a very strong, beautiful, black woman. She was a reflection of love. She showed so much kindness, respect, and love to all that she had ever come in contact with. She loved and nourished her children, and she surely honored her husband. Even though my father had other affairs outside of their marriage, she never said anything bad about him to us. She still had respect for him. She used to put him up a plate of food and told the children not to eat it so that whenever he did come home, he would have something to eat. Mom died from cancer, diabetes, and anemia at Wilson Memorial Hospital when I was 14 years old. I was in the ninth grade. I watched her whenever she would get sick from the chemotherapy treatment. My mom said that her doctor said that she had a spot on one of her lungs. The doctor said that it was cancer. I felt really bad whenever she would come back from chemotherapy because she would be severely sick on her stomach. Mom started losing weight. She lost all of her lovely grey hair. She was hospitalized, and she got better before she died. Her hair had been growing back. We thought that she was on her way back home, but unfortunately before we were about to go to the hospital to bring her home, she passed away. We got a phone call from my aunt, the late Dorothy Barnes Williams, saying that she had passed away. I know that she is up in heaven because she accepted Jesus as her personal Savior and she was lying in her casket with a smile on her face.

Mom was an excellent cook. She would make a pan of biscuits that would melt in your mouth. Sometimes, I would just take a biscuit and get me a cool glass of Kool-Aid and just lay back and enjoy the flavor. I remembered the aroma of her southern fried chicken, fat back meat, and biscuit pudding. Oh my goodness, everything that she cooked was ummmmmmm good. Every Friday afternoon whenever I got off the school bus, I could smell the aroma of her cooking some fried fish and cornbread.

One sure thing that I will never forget is how a live chicken that I used to feed ended up on our kitchen table. I will never forget whenever my mom used to ring the chicken's neck. That chicken would be hopping and twirling around in the yard. She would get an axe and chop its head off. Then she would bring some hot, boiling water outside to pluck the feathers off of the chicken. I helped her. It was amazing to me. The children of today would probably turn up their noses at the food that we used to eat back in the day. Whenever I growing up, we ate chickens from off our on yard, pigs that we had raised squirrels, rabbits, birds, fish, and all kinds of food that some of the children of today wouldn't consider eating.

My parents not only took care of us, but they took care of some of our cousins too. Some of our cousins would spend the entire summer with us. They helped my parents work on the farm by putting into tobacco.

My father, the late Willie James Lofton was a people person. He was half Cherokee Indian. I do not believe that he had ever met a stranger. He loved to have parties too. Sometimes he would cook a pig on a big grill all night and we would have a great crowd of people over at our house the next day. Family, neighbors, and friends were always welcome at our house. I really do not know a whole lot about my dad because he left mom whenever I was in the 5th grade. That didn't stop me from loving him. My brother and pastor, the late Kenneth Lee Lofton, taught us to honor who are parents are. We don't have to honor what they have done wrong, but we can honor who they are because they gave birth to us. **Ephesian 6:1–3 "Children, obey your parents in the Lord: for this is right. Honour thy father and mother; which is the first commandment with promise: That it may be well with thee, and thou mayest live long on the earth."**

On the farm we didn't only barn tobacco and pick up cucumbers. We also had a couple of gardens. We picked up potatoes in the field, and the garden was filled with fresh vegetables. We had apples trees and peach trees. We grew juicy watermelons that where so big at times that a child couldn't tote one by his or herself. I believe it is not true whenever older people said that young people don't have a back but they only have gristle. I would like to know what was it that was hurting me while I was picking those cucumbers.

I know it seems a little strange for someone that was my age to say this, but I had really enjoyed getting up at around 4 o'clock every morning during the summer time. I was picking cucumbers at the age of five years old. I also packed tobacco at that age. Sometimes my mom would let me lay the tobacco sticks on the looping machine. She would let me stand on a tall brick at the looping machine and I would place the tobacco stick on the tobacco. The best thing about putting in tobacco was break time. I loved those icy cold crush grape and crush orange sodas. I loved pouring peanuts in a good old Pepsi or Coca Cola! Ahhhhh, it was so good! It was yummy to my tummy! And the honey buns were very delicious.

By the time that I was about 13 years old, I was helping my late Uncle John and late Aunt Bessie Barnes hand tobacco. It wasn't hard working in tobacco. I just hated to see those fat, green, slimy tobacco worms. I felt good making my own paycheck too.

Picking up cucumbers wasn't hard to do unless I had seen a frog hopping across my fingers. I almost pee peed on myself one day whenever I had seen a slithering snake in the cucumber field. Seeing snakes made me want to pack up and leave the field.

Family Life is so important. Our family really enjoyed one another. We loved it whenever my dad used to take all of us fishing. I could really dig up some fishing worms. At first, I was very scared because the big fishing worms wiggled so much that I thought that they were baby snakes. I soon loved digging up the fishing worms in our own back yard alongside of my big brothers. Right now even today, I still enjoy fishing.

Family life was also great whenever my dad used to get all of us to entertain his company. His drinking buddies would come over to the house, and we were sometimes the entertainment. I think that is why everyone in my family can sing and dance. Dad used to give us money to dance for them. Oh, what great times, listening to the oldies but goodies! I loved the slow jams like: Marvin Gay,

Teddy Pendergrass, Barry White, Aretha Franklin, Gladys Knight, the Temptations, and especially The Jackson Five. I loved a lot more artists as well. I thought sure that Michael Jackson and I were going to grow up to get married. Well, so much for my childhood fantasies.

My family sometimes got in the backyard and played soft ball, kickball, and some other activities. We used to hate if someone knocked the ball too hard and we had to go to the pig pin in order to get it. Oh, what fun we had. I believe that the activities that we had really kept us in good shape. I especially liked hop scotch. We used to have so much fun. I can't play it like I used to because I am a little too fluffy. By me being fluffy and the side effects from Covid 19, I have to play games that don't involve too much jumping and running.

As a child, I would go into the backyard, look up at the sun, and talk with God. I always asked Him whether or not He was real. Today, I don't have to ask Him that because I know without a shadow of a doubt that God is real. The word of God Almighty is fulfilling itself. The signs of the end times are found in the word of God according to **Matthew 24:3–31.**

Sometimes, I would just go in my backyard and sing. My neighbor, Pastor Jeffrey Sims, could hear the echoes of me singing from my house all the way up the path. I love singing. I would sing gospel, the slow jams, and I would just sing whatever came into my mind.

These experiences that I had when I was small, I believe that it made me appreciate all that God had blessed me with and what He shall continue to bless me with. There were good and not so good times in my life while I was growing up. If I had listened to the wisdom of most of the older people, I could have saved myself less hard aches and pains.

Schools That I've Attended

THE SCHOOLS THAT I've attended are Lucama Elementary, Springfield Middle, and Hunt High. Whenever I moved to Wilson, I had attended Fike High School. Whenever I went to Durham, North Carolina, I had graduated from Hillside High School, but I took a Cosmetology class at Durham High. I had attended Kittrell Job Corps, Vance Granville Community College, and the JTPA program through Durham Technical Institute. The last two colleges that I had attended were Ashford University and Liberty University.

I began school in the 1st grade at Lucama Elementary School located in Lucama, NC. I really love this school. At the time that I went to school at Lucama, it was also a high school. Therefore, my older siblings were also there, the late Jesse Lee Lofton and Frostina Lofton Renfrow.

I used to enjoy the afternoons at school whenever the students would go out and play activities on the playground. We played kick ball, dodge ball, soft ball, and we also had monkey bars. Soon after we came in from the playground, it was almost time to go home.

One of the best teachers that I've ever had was Mrs. Tomlinson. I had her for the 2nd and the 5th grades. She taught us well, and she was concerned about us learning. I hope that she's still alive today. I saw her at Parker's Barbecue in 2009. I also love my teacher Mrs. Gwendolyn Speight McNeil. She was my teacher in the 8th grade at the old Springfield Middle School.

I loved the Christmas parties that we used to have in school. Lucama Elementary was the place where it was my first time seeing a live Santa Claus. I was so excited. Santa also had some helpers. It just seems like those old times were the best days of my life. I had even imagined one Christmas that I had heard Santa on my roof.

Lucama Elementary is still standing today. I still remember when I was around nine and ten how we used to get lots of snow. I remember on one occasion when the school bus was coming, and I had to run down that long path. I believe now the address is 6101 Blalock Road in Lucama, NC. While I was running on this particular day, there was still ice down the path after it had snowed. Before I had gotten to the bus stop, I had fallen down several times. By the time I had gotten on the school bus, I had a big busted lip where I had fallen. The children laughed at me so hard that I started crying. My brother, Kenneth still laughed about it whenever he was living.

I remember one time I tried to skip school. Lord, how mercy! I missed the bus on purpose. I might have missed the bus because I either didn't do my homework, or I didn't study for my test. Anyway, my mom, Tenie Mae, she could see right through me. How about this, she walked me all the way to school that day. You know, I didn't miss the bus on purpose anymore. I had learned my lesson. I was already a chubby little girl. That walk, honey, put something on me!

I went to Springfield Middle School from the sixth to the eighth grade. I really do not recall much. I do remember when I was in the sixth grade. I had an accident at home. I got burnt by some hot boiling water. In order for us to have baths, we had to boil our water on the stove. One particular morning, I went to pour the pot full of boiling water into my foot tub. Suddenly, the entire pot fell backwards on me. You would have thought that I was Koonta Kentae getting my foot chopped off. My sister, still today talks about the horrible scream that I made, and how it looked like I was tap dancing. My mom had to call my Uncle John Barnes to rush me to the hospital. I love my mom, but what made her put Vicks vapor rub on me, I do not know. When they threw the sheets over me at the hospital, I felt like I was in a hell burning. I was crying like I was in a flame of fire. I had to stay out of school a couple of weeks, but eventually I healed wonderfully by the grace of God. Prayer and Cocoa butter really does wonders.

There is one time that my mom asked me to go the neighbor's house to stand and wait for the school bus. She had never asked me to do that. That's how I know that obedience is better than sacrifice. **I Samuel 15:22 "And Samuel said, Hath the Lord as great delight in burnt offerings and sacrifices, as in obeying the voice of the Lord? Behold, to obey is better than sacrifice, and to hearken than the fat of rams."** It was raining cats and dogs. A few minutes after I went to the neighbor's house, a car came by and hydroplaned and knocked over our mail box. I usually stood right beside the mailbox to catch the school bus. It was God's angels watching over me, I do believe. If I hadn't been obedient that day to my mom, the car would have probably ripped my head from my body. Thank you God for sparing my life!

While I was in the ninth grade, my mom had died. We had ended up moving from Lucama to Wilson. The only best thing about that move to me was having an inside bathroom. Our outhouse was about to cave in. Plus, I was afraid to sit in the outhouse because I was scared that a snake would be lurking around and it would bite me on my butt.

I soon began to attend Fike High School. I had attended Fike High School for almost two years. After my mom died, my brothers took care of me. We all lived in an apartment on Vance Street for a while. My brothers soon began to have their individual's apartments. I still remain with my brother, Kenneth, and his wife, Helen Cox Lofton. Soon my brother decided to go into the army. I wasn't able to go with them. I do not know what was wrong with me, but I was in my teenage years, and I didn't want to be obedient. When I was told that I wasn't able to go with them, I ran away from home. I didn't want to go stay with my dad and his new wife, Diane. It wasn't that she would treat me bad, I was just afraid and I was fearful of life itself.

Whenever I ran away, I ran to one of the houses that belonged to a brother and his wife from our church, Trinity Deliverance Center. I asked him not to tell where I was. Soon, I saw my brother and sister come through his door. My sister Frostina from Durham and her husband, Harold took me back to Durham with them. I was so afraid. I didn't know what to do. I ended up graduating from Hillside High School in Durham, North Carolina. I was even an honor roll student.

Running away and having a bad attitude problem might seemed like it was cute, but it wasn't cute. I believe that if I had been more obedient whenever I was young, I would have been able to have had even more better opportunities sooner in life. God is a kind of God that gives anybody that asks Him another chance. I thank God that the work that He had begun in me, He is able to also fulfill it through me and in me. **Philippians 1:6 "being confident of this very thing, that he which hath begun a good work in**

you will perform it until the day of Jesus Christ:" I've made so many mistakes growing up. Mankind sometimes stamps people out, but God can make the nothing that we are and make us to be someone beautiful in Christ Jesus. There's a scripture in the Bible that says that we are wonderfully and beautifully made. God loves all of us, and He wants us to give ourselves unto Him so that He can use us for His glory.

I believe sometimes we expect the worst out of situations. I believe that if we trust God with all of our heart, we will always know that no matter what comes our way, God is on our side. God always knows what is best for us. He cares for us, whether or not it's through our good times or not so good times. God has never let us down. God is sovereign and He never makes a mistake. Whenever sorrow comes, the devil brings it into our lives.

After I graduated in June 1987 from high school, I signed up for Kittrell Job Corps. I left for Kittrell Job Corps in September of 1987. My intentions whenever I got out of school weren't to go to the Job Corps. I believe I ended up there because of my disobedience. I was too grown to listen to my sister, Frostina and her husband, Harold. I wasn't a bad person. I was just a little hard headed.

My Lord, when I first arrived, I was so afraid because I had heard nothing but bad news about job corps. People told me all the bad things that could happen. It put fear in my heart and I was probably shaking in my boots. My first night was horrible. I couldn't sleep all night. Somebody had told me that all my roommates where lesbians. It was so hard for me to sleep with that butter knife all night long. I didn't realize what was worst, thinking about being attacked or realizing that I could have stabbed myself with that butter knife that I had taken from the cafeteria earlier. Until this day, I do not know if the women were lesbians or not, but I can say that they were always nice and very respectable to me.

Kittrell College paid my way to Vance Granville Community College, where I had graduated from the Cosmetology. When I made the Dean's list a couple of times, I was put in the honor room at the job corps. Instead of me having three roommates, I had just one roommate. Before I had gone to Vance Granville, I had taken Retail Sales at Kittrell. That's when I learned how to do the ten-key strokes.

Kittrell Job Corps was very exciting for me. I feel like it was a great experience. I learned to make up a bunk bed so tight that a nickel could bounce on it. I learned how to clean bathrooms quite well, and I was in charge of supplies. As a student at the job corps, I were given clothing allowances, a small check every two weeks for personal use, and I could also work on campus if I chose to. I had enjoyed going to church every now and then. The staff took us on so many activities. Sometimes we went bowling, skating, to the movies, to concerts, and we went to some amusement parks. There was never a dull moment at the job corps. They had a volleyball net set up outside the Student Union. The Student Union was like a big entertainment area for the students. The students could shoot pool, watch TV, do arts and crafts, and just have a great time. Almost every Friday, Kittrell would have dances in the Student Union. Oh, I could really dance. I would just move to the beat in a sexy kind of way. The way that I moved would say without words, come, dance with me only if you can hang.

I became very good friends with some great people. Some of the people were **Tammy Lowery**, **Diane Harris**, **Amber**, **late Charlene Burch**, and a lot of other beautiful people. We would laugh and just enjoy ourselves.

I really enjoyed myself at Kittrell Job Corps. I give a special thanks to **Mr. Phillip Woods-Reese**, if he is still alive. He had been an encouragement to me while I was at the job corps. I really missed being there sometimes even though I hadn't gone back to ever visit the campus.

In 1992, I had gone to the JTPA associated with Durham Tech in Durham, NC. I took a crash course for Medical Terminology and Office Procedures. Going through this program had opened up an opportunity for me to work for the County of Durham in the Purchasing Department in 1992.

In 2006, I began my curriculum at Wilson Community College in the Community Spanish Interpreter Program. I am not fluent. I wished that I were fluent. Nevertheless, the Spanish language is so beautiful to me. I really love their culture also, and I do have Hispanics that are married into my family. There were so many days that I were going to school feeling rough, but I still had pressed my way. I felt like I couldn't give up. I wanted to finish my curriculum. I thank my teacher **Mr. John Robinson** for making Spanish an interesting class. He was an inspiration to me, and he is very fluent with this language.

I graduated from Ashford University with a bachelor's degree in Organizational Management and a master's degree in teaching Adult Literacy. I am two classes from having a doctorate degree from Liberty University. My doctorate's degree is in Strategic Leadership.

THREE

I Tried to Commit Suicide

I BELIEVE THAT the teenager stage may be the roughest and the toughest. We as young ladies and guys try to tell mom and dad how grown up we are. We start smelling our own tails, our own musk, as the older people would say.

I had heard about other girls having a boyfriend. I wanted to have a boyfriend too. So a friend of mine, Barbara, introduced me to Clarence. Clarence would come to visit me. Back then, we stayed down a long, dirt path in Lucama, North Carolina. First, we had gone to the county fair together. Everything was cool with us. Well one day, I went over to his house. He had family members that were home. I think that her and her kids went somewhere for a little while. I wished that I wouldn't have given up my virginity until I had gotten married.

That was my first time having sexual intercourse. I was a virgin, I said, "What are you doing to me. What hole are you searching for? You are about to kill me." He stopped, because he knew I wasn't going for that. Well he tried again. It was rough for me, by it being my first time. Now, you know once the 1st time is over, sex feels a little better the second time around. Listen, I didn't say that sex wasn't good. What I am saying is that I wished that I had saved myself for my husband. This boy, he didn't love me. It was all about the bootie. We need more people encouraging the younger people about absentness until he or she gets married. Being a virgin whenever an individual gets married isn't anything to be ashamed of. It's an honorable thing. God doesn't desire for an individual to have sex before marriage. Every time an unmarried person sleeps together with another individual they become one person with that individual that he or she sleeps with. **I Corinthians 6:16 "What? Know ye not that he which is joined to an harlot is one body? For two, saith he, shall be one flesh."**

Even though I had sex before marriage, I had to allow Jesus to wash me in His blood. I know that I am forgiven. I've asked Jesus to come into my life. Now, as long as I know that Jesus has forgiven me that is the only thing that matters. It's what God says about any of us that ever count.

Shortly afterward, we broke up, and I ended up taking about a half bottle full of aspirins. I didn't die, but I got something called "the mad itch." I had promised myself that I will never ever attempt suicide again, even though the devil tries to suggest that to me, whenever I am going through my trials and tribulations, Satan wants me to have a pity party for myself. He wants me to feel as though nobody cares for me. I want each and everyone to know that God cares about us. Even if mankind doesn't seem to care about you, know that God does. By knowing that God cares about us, it's very comforting to me. There's an excellent book to read about suicide. It's called **"Driven to the Edge: A Biblical Examination of Suicide" by Randy Raynes.** I don't want to commit suicide and then let it be like a domino effect to my children, family, or friends. I have to trust God through the good times and tough times in my life. **I Peter 5:7 "Casting all your care upon him; for he careth for you."**

Well, I told the Lord, "This day Lord, I want to be with you." It is so amazing when we are young how we are not afraid of death, but as we get older, we are a little uneasy about death. I know for a fact that whenever I die in this day and time that I will be with God. To be absent from the body is to be present with the Lord, according to what is written in the word of God. **Hebrew 9:27–28 "And as it is appointed unto men once to die, but after this the judgment: So Christ was once offered to bear the sins of man; and unto them that look for him shall he appear the second time without sin unto salvation."**

A couple of years ago, I had so many panic attacks, because I didn't want to die. The panic attacks were so severe. They felt as though I was having a heart attack. I could feel heat rush up the back of my legs. I would break out in a sweat at times, and sometimes it felt as though my tongue was numb. Also, my fingers and hands felt like they were tingling.

I found out in the Word of God that God says that we are wonderfully and beautifully made. He doesn't want us to take our own life. He has created us in His own image. God has a plan for all of us. We are important to Him. **Psalm 139:14 "I will praise thee; for I am fearfully and wonde4rfully made: marvelous are thy works; and that my soul knoweth right well."** It may get rough at times, but I want to finish out any assignment that God has for me, and I would like to encourage you to do the same. Nobody can do the assignment that God has given you to do while on this earth. Let's keep praying, fasting, and meditating on God's word so that we will not abort our assignments from the Lord God Almighty.

FOUR

Positive and Negative Peer Pressure

IN LIFE THERE is positive and negative peer pressure. Positive peer pressure is when others influenced an individual to go in the right direction and make righteous decisions. Negative peer pressure occurs whenever others influenced an individual to go into any negative directions other than the right things that an individual has been taught. Sometimes deep inside an individual he or she has something that is called a gut feeling. A person often knows when people are leading him or her in the wrong directions. Most of the time those gut feelings are right. Sometimes those wrong moves and decisions in life come back to bite us later on.

We have to always remember what the word of God tells us about reaping and sowing. It's so true. Whatever we sow, we also reap. **Galatians 6:7–8 "Be not deceived: God is not mocked: for whatsoever man soweth, that shall he also reap. For he that soweth to his flesh shall of the flesh reap corruption: but he that soweth to the Spirit shall of the Spirit reap life everlasting."** In other words, some of the problems that we suffer from are due to some of the decisions that we have done from the past. In the Bible, King David messed up whenever he had slept with Bathsheba. Please read **II Samuel 11–12; I Kings Chapters 1–2**. Although he repented, the sword never left his house. So many bad things were happening in his life and in the life of his children.

I know from experience that surrounding oneself around the right people could really make a difference in a person's life. I want to always surround myself around people that want something out of life. I do not want to surround myself around people that have activities that could lead me to an early grave or to a burning hell. I believe in living my life to the fullest.

I want to let the word of God be my greatest influence. I want to hear the voice of God. I want to allow His Spirit and His word to lead and guide me every day of my life. I know that if I follow the voice of the Holy Spirit that I can make it through this life's journey. I'll prosper; I'll have good success, and there is no limit to the blessings that He has in store for me not only on this earth, but even after death. I know that I have a reward waiting for me up in heaven whenever I get there. **Matthew 6:19–21 "Lay not up for yourselves treasure upon earth, where moth and rust doth corrupt, and where thieves break through and steal: But lay up for yourselves treasures in heaven, where neither moth nor rust doth corrupt, and where thieves do not break through nor steal: For where your treasure is, there will your heart be also."**

FIVE

Dreams, They Do Come True

I BELIEVE THAT dreams come true. I will never forget that whenever I attended elementary school that I told a girl named Angela that I wanted to become a professional singer. She said, "Keep dreaming because it will never happen." Oh, my dream was crushed right then and there. Sometimes we need to be careful about what comes out of our mouths. We also need to be careful to guard our ears, eyes, and our hearts from others that have no dreams. Sometimes, we can let words that come from people that do not know God destroy our dreams, passions, and destiny. **Proverbs 18:21 "Death and life are in the power of the tongue; and they that love it shall eat the fruit thereof."**

Solid Rock Ministries' gospel Cd has been finished for almost five years. The Lord blessed me to write three original songs on the CD project. **Prophet Calvin Suggs** that owns **106.9 FM** produced the music at his radio station here in Wilson, NC on Airport Road for Solid Rock Ministries. My three songs are "**Forgive Me**", "**Majesty**", and **Hallelujah is the Highest Praise** aka "**Hallelujah**". My brother, the late Kenneth Lee Lofton has four original songs that he had written, and my niece's group called "**One Way Up**" has three original gospel raps songs on the CD project. Whenever my brother passed away, the project had been delayed. Yet, I pray that it can be released in 2025 with God's help. I am not going to let my passion and dream die any longer. God has given me the ability to sing this gospel and that's what I intend to do. Whenever I sing, joy, peace, and God's love comes from within me. I put my entire heart into it. God has given each and every one of us talents and gifts to be used for His glory. Though we grow old, we are never too old to be used by God. Please, don't let your dreams die.

I got tired of talking about what I wanted to do in life. I have been talking about a gospel CD project for so many years. I had to get up and do something. My pastor and brother, the late Kenneth Lofton had always told the congregation, "If what you're doing isn't working, get up and try something new."

It's time to stop listening to the negative things that someone has said about you. Mankind has sometimes said what you couldn't do and what you'll never be able to do. It's time to listen to what God has said that you can be and do through His word. In order to know the promises of God Almighty and what He has said, one must first pray, seek the face of God, read, and meditate on the word of God for his or herself. For all that can't read, the word of God is now on online, CD's, DVD's, Bible apps, and etc. I let the Bible app read to me every night while I am sleeping. The word of God and worship music brings a sense of peace into my home, heart, soul, and spirit.

SIX

My Son and Grandson

I TRULY THANK God for my son, Timothy and my grandson, Tyrran. I could never have children. Ummmmmmmh, that's what I thought. In 1990 about two months before I got pregnant, I asked the Lord for a child. I wanted a son. I had tried for hears to have a child, and I couldn't. After I asked God to bless me with my son, two months later, I had gotten pregnant. I wanted to have at least one descendent to leave behind on this universe.

The exciting part was that I didn't get but two monthly, regular cycles that year. Whenever I did get a monthly cycle, it would stay for about five to six weeks. I used to feel so drain and worn down whenever I had a cycle that stayed on that long.

Nevertheless, my son's father kept getting extremely sick on his stomach. I didn't have any symptoms at all. He begged me to go to the doctor. I had finally gone to the Pregnancy Support Center in Durham, North Carolina. My friend, Charlene, kept saying that I was pregnant and my son's father was also telling me the same thing. Pregnancy was the best experience that I could ever have gone through. I had a magnificent pregnancy. I hardly ever got sick on the stomach. I ate almost anything that I wanted. I could gobble down a lot of iced, cold milk. The only food that made me sick was greasy pizza. I ate fish almost every day, because my sister-in-law, Patricia Manning aka Dee, and her friend went fishing all the time. They use to catch some humongous catch fish and my Dee would fry catch fish nuggets for us almost every day.

On July 10, 1991 my water broke after 12 midnight. I bent down to sit on the toilet. I heard something pop like a balloon. A few minutes later, I felt the pain. I never had any back pain. That pain wasn't in my stomach. It was in my private area only. I was hurting so bad, I felt like Fred Sanford on Sanford and Son. He used to say, "I'm coming to join you Elisabeth." I wasn't going to join Elisabeth, but I felt like I was going to be with the Lord. My sister, Frostina and my sister-in-law tried to comfort me. My sister wiped my face with a damp cloth. I took the cloth and threw it across the room. I think I did that after they cut my epidermal off so that I could feel the labor pains in order to know when I needed to push. Oooops that was the wrong thing for them to have done for me! They had to call in more doctors. One time, I had grabbed the doctor by the tie and I said, "Please help me, I need a caesarean." The doctor said that if I had pushed my son out that it would have disfigured his entire face. My son, he just had an extra-large head. I had pushed, strained, pushed, and I was suctioned also. They finally had to give me a C-section. My son was born July 11, 1991. Timothy Jr. was 7 lbs. and 12 ounces, but his head was the biggest thing on his body. I felt like I was holding an extra-large baby doll instead of a newborn. I was desperately afraid though. I had never taken care of a child before. I was so protected over him. I wanted to keep him safe. As he began to get bigger, I would let him go more places. I heard about so much child abuse in our society, so I was careful about the places that I had allowed him to go.

I love him and I want the best for him. I want my son, most of all, to receive the fullness of God. I want him to know Jesus as his personal Savior. I try to teach him the right way to go. Every individual has to choose Christ for him or herself. I am so proud of him. He works with the State of North Carolina. He builds stereo boxes. He used to experiment with electronics at an early age. He used to ask for anything that he could tinkle with. He really has some great ideas. I just let him know one thing. I told him to be very careful not to set my hair on fire. I told him that jerry curls and hair with chemical on it catches on fire really quickly.

I pray that he'll be what God would like for him to be. I praise God because he had blessed my son not to need seizure medications any more. At one time, he had very bad seizures. I used to pray to God for his healing. I thank God that today, he doesn't need it. Thank you Jesus for your healing, **Isaiah 53:4–5 "Surely he hath borne our griefs, and carried our sorrow: yet we did esteem him stricken, smitten of God, and afflicted. But he was wounded for our transgressions; he was bruised for our iniquities: the chastisement of our peace was upon him; and with his stripes we are healed."**

I wanted to always do what the word of God says to do about training up your children in the ways of the Lord. **Proverbs 22:6 "Train up a child in the way he should go: And when he is old, he will not depart from it."** Even though I had strayed away from God, I came back to God because of my teachings when I first gave my life to God, which was at the age of 13. Now, since my son Timothy has a son, my 15 year old grandson, Tyrran, I take him to church and talk to him about God as well. Tyrran wants to be a basketball player. He's a good kid even though he used to be a little stubborn at times. Yet, he is my sweetheart. I pray that I get a chance to watch him graduate from high school, begin his career, and have children of his own someday.

SEVEN

I Wish I Were a Virgin When I Got Married

SOMETIMES HABITS ARE so hard to break once you have started them. I gave up my virginity at the age of 13 years old. It was a terrible idea to do that. I really wished that I had saved myself for marriage.

I remember when my friend, Barbara introduced me to one of her friends. He was an older guy. My cousin, Minnie Ruth Blue spent the night with us one night. At that time, we had an outhouse in the backyard. We had to go use the bathroom outside. Our house was down a long, long path. The guy, Reginald, said, "I'll cut off the lights and you'll have to come out to meet me, okay?" I said, "Alright." That was a stupid mistake. Night came. I received the phone call. I sneaked out of the house and went down that long, dark path to meet Reginald. I kept asking him, "What time is it?" Finally, he took me back home, because I kept asking him about the time. It seemed as though I were only gone a couple of minutes. How about I was gone a couple of hours!

My cousin, Minnie Ruth kept saying out loud, "It's sure taking Geneva a long time to sh*t." My brother said that she kept saying

26

it over and over while I was gone. Oh, my God, I was so busted. Whenever I got back home, the back door was locked. I peeked through the window and seen my brother, Kenneth studying the word of God at our kitchen table. I tried to knock lightly so that only he could hear me. I knock gently on the door. My brother let me in. How about in the old houses, boards in the floor made plenty of screeching noises.

I almost got to my bed. My mom yelled, "Geneva, where have you been?" I thought that my mom was going to kill me. She was asking me all kinds of questions. She had asked me whether or not I was hurt, pregnant, and all kinds of questions. I believe that I was hurting inside more than what she was hurting. I heard the sniffling in her sweet voice. Deep down inside, she felt like tearing my tail up, but she was so concerned about me coming back home safe and sound.

I had a great mom, not because she didn't tear my tail up that night, but because she always did her best to provide for us and keep us safe. She did the best that she could after dad had left us. My mom could have been rough with me. My mom, Tenie Mae Barnes Lofton, she wouldn't stop whooping your butt until she stopped talking. That weeping willow tree that was in our front yard wasn't only for the good shade. The tree's branches were at times broken, twisted together, and plaited for a rod of correction. Her whooping me the correct way, made me love her even more. She didn't abuse me, but she spanked me real good at times.

Mom used to pick cucumbers, barn tobacco, plant a garden, plant flowers, chop wood, and she just took really good care of all of us. Sometimes I felt as though she should have had the opportunity for others to take better care of her. I wished all the times that I were more obedient. Whenever someone is gone, it's too late to be obedient and good to them. I did learn from some of my mistakes and I tried to be obedient and respectful to others. Those of you that have your parents now, it's not too late to be obedient and respectful to them. Give them their roses while they are alive.

I think that it is something wonderful to have two people that are virgins to come together in holy matrimony. If you are a female or a male that have your virginity, please do not give that up for any reasons at all. It is an honor to be a virgin. There's something wrong with the people that may look down on you for wanting to have something pure and untouched to bring to your marriage. For all of us that aren't virgins, we are still someone beautiful through Christ Jesus. He does wash us and cleanse us from within with His blood. We are not to keep downing ourselves. There's no need to keep crying over the spilled milk. I just wanted to encourage those that are still virgins to be proud of it.

EIGHT

I Let My Rape Victim Convince Me that He Loved Me

THERE ARE SO many issues to deal with whenever one is a rape victim. You feel dirty, you're uncomfortable being around men alone, you blame yourself, you have to forgive, and you have to get healing from within. Whether it is through a Rape Support Center, through Christ, healing is there if the victim will reach out for that help.

I used to work at the Compri Hotel in Research Triangle Park, North Carolina. I worked at the Compri Hotel in 1989, if I am not mistaken. I used to clean hotel rooms. I remember Connie E. Oh honey child, he had the cold, black and silky hair. His skin was as smooth as a baby's bottom. Whenever he would walk by me, oh, I believe I was hypnotized at the very site of him like a teenager girl in high school. I should have been worshipping only Jesus. I did not drive at this time in my life, even though I had my driver's license. I was too afraid to drive, and I didn't have a vehicle at the time. I thought that Connie was a little interested in me. He asked whether he could give me a lift to my house. I was so excited that he would want to talk to me. On the way to him dropping me off at my house, he said that he had to stop by his house for a moment. He asked me to come in for a little while. He said that his mom was home. I thought that it would be okay. I was in the front room and his mom was in the back room.

Whenever he went to his own room, after a few minutes, he called me back there. He said, "Geneva, I want you to see something on TV. Come here for a moment." After I entered the room, I had seen where he was playing a pornographic sex tape. I heard the door click behind me. He locked the door so that I couldn't leave. The next thing I could remember, He just pulled at my pants. He didn't give me a kiss. He didn't ask permission to enter. He was taller than I was. He jacked my legs straight up in the air, my head was upside down on the mattress, and my paints were down. He was entering in. I just couldn't do anything. I was so shocked and I was unable to move.

Afterwards, he just said, "Okay, I will take you home now." I was still in shock. I was naïve. I didn't realize that I was a rape victim. The next day, I told my friend, Becky what had happen. She wanted me to go to the police. I was nervous and scared. I was the kind of person that I hated to see bad things happen to people. I should have gone to the police. He didn't call it as rape. He convinced me that we were a couple. How crazy was this. I think that I had overcome the bad, by convincing myself that is wasn't rape to avoid reality. If I only knew back then what I know now, his butt would had been thrown behind bars.

I was acting so naïve. We started seeing each other. I felt like Luke and Laura from the soap opera "General Hospital." How can somebody be raped and then start having a relationship together? I was in denial. You know, I blamed myself over and over and over, so many times. I shouldn't have trusted this stranger. I was a predator for him. I had just finished up at Kittrell Job Corps a couple of months before I started working at the Compri Hotel. Therefore, I had a couple of hundreds saved up. Also, my sister Frostina and her husband had a nice piece of change set aside for me in the bank. I was getting a welfare check after mom had died, and they had saved some of it for me.

I asked myself today, "How did I let this man make a complete fool out of me?" I spent all of my little savings. Most of it, he had stolen from me. I didn't know that he was on drugs. I tell you, anytime someone would say that their mother has died in order to keep a job, you better be aware of them. Connie and I had worked at the same job. When the Compri van picked me up, the maintenance man said, "We're so sorry to hear about the death of your friend's mom. I said, "What happened, who died?" I asked him, "When did she die, because I had just seen his mom at home this morning."

Later, his mom went to stay in another state. She had left us the apartment. We couldn't afford it because of his drug use. I got tired and began to rent me a room inside a rooming house. He stayed with one of his African friends.

I like the rooming house a lot. My only problem was the fact that one of the gentlemen that didn't work was home at all times. He was stealing food. I can't prove that he did it, but my food money got missing. I hid forty dollars underneath my mattress for my food. I believe that he broke into my room and stole my money. I had ended up having only 2 loaves of bread for two entire weeks. God is the only one that sustained me. I was too ashamed to tell anyone that I only had two loaves of bread.

I had always wondered why Connie E. had a pretty woman's picture on his key chain. He said that it was his niece's picture. Well, I come to find out that it was his girlfriend's picture. Wait one moment, it got even crazier than that. I had found out that it was a cousin of mine that I had never seen before. I remind you that my hometown is in Wilson County. I was working in Durham. When my sister went to our family reunion on the Roundtree's side of the family, she was wondering why my boyfriend was there without me. That's when we realized that the girl on the keychain was my cousin. My sister and I laughed constantly for a long time about that. What are the odds of that? I left his butt alone. I didn't have anything to do with him after that.

I really want to tell you something serious. By me being raped, for a long time, I couldn't stand to be alone with any man. That even was true for my own brothers. I know that they wouldn't ever harm me, but every time I heard a door being locked behind me, I was very uncomfortable. I would break out in a sweat, and I would begin to panic.

For every raped victim, I say to you that I feel your pain and your fear. I am so sorry that it happened to you. Please, stop blaming yourselves and let's get our healing through Christ, so that we can go own with our lives.

Hearing the click from someone locking a door taunted me for a while. I still yet remember when I had a nervous breakdown in 2004 and 2005. Whenever that nurse clicked the door behind me on that mental ward, I thought that all hope was lost. I said, "Lord, they're going to keep me here forever." God is yet still helping me to overcome. Without Christ, I couldn't have made it. Surely, now more than ever, I know that today, with Christ, I can make it.

I forgave Him. I had to go own. I believe whenever we forgive people for what he, she or they have done to us, it helps us to go own and it helps us to heal. Now, I never want to put myself in a predicament to be raped again. I will take precautions for myself. I do know that when a person has been raped that it takes time to heal. When I was raped, I felt hopeless, dirty, scared, and I blamed myself. Nevertheless, Jesus is the person that I look to for my complete healing and deliverance. He comforts me and keeps me in my right mind. **Isaiah 26:3 "Thou wilt keep him in perfect peace, whose mind is stayed on thee: because he trusteth in thee."**

NINE

My Divorce of My First Marriage

MY SON'S FATHER, Timothy Jerome Manning Sr., and I met through my friend Becky. Her boyfriend, Mike had introduced us to one another. We got married in November 1993. I believe now, with all of my heart that I shouldn't have gotten married to him. I wanted my son to have his father with us in our home. We were already having problems before we got married.

I kept asking Timothy whether or not he wanted to get married because I felt like I was tired of living in sin. I was sleeping with him without being married to him. I really wanted to return back home because he didn't really want to get married. He threatened me and told me that I wasn't going to take his son nowhere. Then that's when he popped the question. Please, marry me. We shouldn't have gotten married. I believe he wanted me to marry him in order to keep his son close to him. I can honestly say that my son's father loved him.

Timothy Sr. was a nice person. When we got married, he had already been a diabetic ever since the age of nine. I knew that he was sick. I really believe that I got frustrated with him. I was upset and worried about him all of the time. Every time that I went to work, I used to beg him every morning to get up and take his medications. He would fuss about me bugging him to take his medications.

Timothy Sr. had lots of friends. He had male and female friends that he hung out with. I didn't like him hanging out with them most of the times. I was left at home a lot of weekends because I didn't drink and party like some of them partied. It's as if they weren't considerate that he was married and needed to spend time with his wife.

I still remember one night whenever he left my son and me at home. My son was about one year old. We weren't married yet. I heard footsteps in the house, and I thought it was Tim coming back to the house. I had looked up suddenly, I looked up and seen a shadow in the formed of an older man. I could hear and see the old man walking. He walked into the room where my baby would have been laying. I just grabbed Timothy Jr, and started pleading the blood of Jesus! I didn't know anything else until I woke up the next morning. We had to end up leaving that house on E. Club Blvd. The TV started cutting off by itself. I told his father that he could stay, but I was leaving. That place had a spirit in it.

I believe that I was frustrated with a few of his female friends. One night, I went completely off whenever I had seen one of his female friends dropping him off at 10pm. I was so mad. I broke the screen door and all trying to see what was going on. He used to work on some of his ex-girlfriend's vehicles during the day while I was away at work. I was jealous and my heart didn't trust him like I should have trusted him.

I wasn't any peaches and cream myself, but he would come to the job sometimes and pretended he needed money to fix the car whenever he really hadn't fixed anything. Soon, on my job at

LabCorp, I began to work 12 hours a day at times. I felt some days that I shouldn't have to work 12 hours and have to come home to cook, and be able to please him every night. Later, I wanted to pack up and leave. We were always in need and I felt like I was working as hard as I could. I believe that we should have been in church, getting some counseling. A couple of months later, my mind just wandered in another direction. I wanted to get out of my marriage. I felt tired and frustrated. He always reminded me of how he wanted my hair and clothes to be neat like his older son's mom, but every dime that I made was spent trying to keep a roof over our heads. If I was in the Lord then like I am now, who knows, our marriage could had survived. The only way I knew at that time was to get a divorce. Timothy Sr. was a nice person. Sometimes he was stuck in his ways.

I think that I was worried about life too much. I kept worrying about how I was going to make it, about my husband's health, about my child, and just about everything. I believe that's the reason behind me developing anxiety attacks. One night, I woke from a deep sleep. I was trying to grab my shoulders. I felt my spirit was trying to come up out of my body. I was so terrified. My spirit was actually trying to leave my body, even after I had awakened for a couple of seconds. My spirit man was trying to go upward.

I had severe panic attacks at Labcorp. While I was working, I could feel heat rushing up the back of my legs, my tongue would get very numb, and I would have shortness of breath. My boss, Cora, explained to the paramedics that it looked as if my eyes were rolling back in the back of my head. Till this day, I believe that they weren't panic attacks. I believe I was getting reading to die due to sleep apnea. I always slept a lot on that job. I would fall asleep a lot of times while I was typing and trying to work, even though I tried my best to stay awake.

I had decided that if I was going to die, I didn't want my son to not know my side of the family. I packed up my belongings and I moved back home to Wilson, North Carolina. Also, I wanted my son to know the Lord. I knew that his father wouldn't pressure him to go to church like I wanted him to go to church. I believed that his father let him get away with little more things than what I would let him get away with.

TEN

The Day I Had an Affair, I Ended My Marriage

WHAT I AM about to tell you, God has already forgiven me. My marriage was so shaky, hanging on by the thinnest thread that one could ever find. One day, I had decided to visit my ex-boyfriend, Ricky, back in Wilson. Well, nothing happened whenever I saw him, at least there wasn't anything that happened the first time. The second time that we met back up was devastating on my behalf. I blamed myself for sleeping with him. Please, do not ever start a fire that can't easily be extinguished.

If two people are having problems in their marriage, neither one of them need to have conversations with their ex's. And their ex's don't ever need to give him or her counsel about their marriage. A spouse should seek out godly counsel in a godly environment. That's how infidelity can begin. In all actually, it would be nice for that husband and wife to get godly counsel together with a pastor and his wife that has a strong married and doesn't mine telling both of them the truth about how to resolve issues, according to the word of God. Those spouses need to spend time together and never take one another for granted. Don't be looking at the grass that seems greener on the other side.

Meanwhile, whenever I went back home, the guilt and shame covered me quickly and I just told my son's father that I couldn't be married to him anymore. The first reason is that I was guilty. I didn't believe in sleeping with several people at the same time. The second reason is that I didn't use protection and just in case I had picked up anything, I didn't want to bring him back any type of diseases. The third reason is that I feared for my life and I were too afraid to tell him that I had slept with another man. He took insulin and I was afraid that he would kill me. He was so mad at me that he grabbed our son and wouldn't let me see him for a couple of days. I called the police, but the police couldn't do anything for me because I didn't have legal custody over him. I was so miserable trying to go to work. My son was the reason, plenty of days, why I wanted to live and not commit suicide. I love my child. He is a precious gift from God to me.

I remember when I first found out that I was pregnant. My son's father and I were not getting alone well. This was before we were married. He asks me to go back to my hometown for a couple of days. I went to stay with my God mother and God father, the late Sherrie Ann Caple Cox Williams and Purvis Williams. Whenever I had returned home, I found a note from one of his female friends saying how much she had enjoyed the weekend with him. When I surprisingly came home, Valerie had stopped by our house. She was surprised to see me. I was barefoot and pregnant. She began to cry and he ran behind her. It amazed me! I thought that I was his only baby girl.

After Valerie left our house, my son's father asked me why I came back. He insisted that I couldn't stay at our house that we had rented together. I was thinking about all that food that was eaten up while I was gone. I had spent my hard earned money paying for. He immediately asked his mom and dad if I could move in with them because I was pregnant with his son. They took me in and had mercy on me. They didn't have to do that.

After I had the baby, I had picked up the telephone one day and caught my ex-husband and Valerie on the telephone talking together. The last words that I heard were that they loved each other. I butted in and said something to let them know that I heard their conversation. I can't remember all the words that were said. The next thing I knew that girl came over to his mom's house. I was shaking in my boots and talking junk from the screen door at the same time. I had just had my baby, I didn't know how to fight, and I wasn't about to go outside to get my butt whooped. My son's father went out to calm her down. If I were a fighter, I would had gone outside and put down a piece of fighting. When you do not know how to fight physically, you better stand back and talk from a distant. I talked really loud because I really wanted everybody to come to my rescue. Now in these days and times, people don't fight fair. They want to shoot you, or even stab you, and let you die.

Sometimes we see the signs before we get married that we aren't marrying the right person. I believe that God sends us warnings ahead of time. If we choose to open up our eyes, ears, and heart unto God and really listen to Him talking to us, we can save ourselves and save that spouse lots of wasted time, heartaches, headaches, money and tremendous pain. Sometimes, we know God told us not to marry somebody, but we do it anyhow. We think that we can change people. We can't change anybody but ourselves. I just know from now on to learn from my mistakes. I need to listen to the Holy Ghost within me that says unsafe or safe. I believe that our marriage had failed not because of one person. It failed because of the both of us were not doing what we ought to have done in our relationship. I believe selfishness on both parties sometimes is some of the reasons why marriages don't last.

I also believe that's why I stayed in the second marriage to an alcoholic and drug addict because I was trying not to have another divorce. I wanted to make sure that I did everything possible in order to keep it together. My first marriage lasted three years. My second marriage had lasted about seven years.

Even though Timothy Sr. and I got a divorce, we were at peace with one another. I always made sure his son saw him whenever he was living. My son usually spent every summer and every holiday with his dad. We made sure that we never forgot his birthday, Father's Day, Christmas, and any other special days that we could acknowledge him. He also spent every summer with the Manning side of the family. His soul is resting in heaven now.

ELEVEN

My Divorce of the Second Marriage

MR. RONNIE SINCLAIR and I got married May, 1999 in Wilson, North Carolina. This was my second marriage. I should have taken more time to heal from the first marriage. I had really learned a good lesson after this second time around. He had several problems with substance abuse. I blame myself because I shouldn't have gotten married. I had seen the signs, but I was trying to convince myself that it was going to get better. I said, "Once this man sees the love that I have for him, he will be happy to let the drugs and alcohol go." How about, you can't change a person's will. I believe sometimes that once you say, "I do", things get even worse at times. Our pastor always said, "One must choose to change, neither you nor the Lord will break a person's will." The warning sign was when we first met. He was living next door to my brother. I asked my brother to ask him if he wanted to go to the movies with me. Well, Ronnie said yes. We didn't even go to the movies; we hung out with my aunt and my cousins in Lucama, North Carolina.

I didn't need to start dating anyone. I needed to rest and heal from my last divorce. After the divorce, I should have let God cleanse me. No, I was hot in my box, and I didn't take time to heal. Sometimes, like I did, a woman or a man chooses people just like the same relationship that he or she came away from. He was doing worse than what was going on in my first marriage. I blame no one but myself. The second warning sign was when he showed up a couple of hours late for the wedding with liquor on his breath. I was so ashamed of being embarrassed that I still went forward with the wedding. I should have done like someone had told me and just let the guest eat the food and go back home. We always pay for the terrible choices that we have made.

Ronnie was on drugs so bad. We had lost our home because he couldn't keep a job. He drank on the job so much that they let him go on almost every job that he worked.

My son and I had to hide our money. Plenty of times food, clothing, video tapes, and so much other things were taken and sold for drugs. I had to sleep with my keys up underneath my pillow or in my bra so that he wouldn't let the drug dealer use my car. Several times, I had to go retrieve my cars from the drug dealers. Sometimes, they would call me on the phone saying how he owed them money. One time after tax season, he brought the drug dealer into my bedroom to collect money for his drug habit. After he had left, when I woke up the next morning, he tried to convince me that I had lost the rest of his money. He came back and stole the rest of the money that was underneath my pillow. Whenever I flipped over, he took the rest. I had to break him down and talk to him until he finally told me that while I was sleeping, he came back for the rest of the money. I don't know how he did it. I must had been really tired for me not to know that he could remove money from up underneath my pillowcase.

One time whenever we stayed in Black Creek, he took a box cutter and cut my pillowcase to get my keys out of my pillow case. I'm so glad that I didn't sneeze or make a move too suddenly. He could have cut my neck by mistake.

When you're in any relationship and that individual is on drugs, it's a very unhealthy relationship. I seldom had peace through this marriage. Individuals that are on drugs do a lot of manipulating things to get his or her way. He or she are very good charmers. Whenever they mess up, they will say I'm sorry so convincing that you'll believe them every time. They are specialist at telling lies.

With my ex-husband, Ronnie, I never knew what he was going to take from us next. I had the tags on my vehicle that was stolen. He says that he didn't do it, but his nephew said he did it. I remembered waking up from a deep sleep and he was standing over me. I swung and kicked up. He immediately said, "Wait, Neva; it's me." I wanted to know why he was standing over me. He said that he was just seeing how beautiful I was sleeping. He was about to get his tail tore up. I never hated my husband because whenever he wasn't out drugging and drinking, we got along so well. Yet, drug- life is very painful to deal with from both the user and the person or people that reach out to help that person get off from substance abuse.

I think the most painful thing was whenever my husband made love to me real good so that I could fall asleep fast, then he would get my car keys and slip out the door. I would wake up after we had made love and reach for him and he would be gone, plenty of times. It made me feel less than a woman. I felt like a first class fool. I was full but yet empty at the same time. My body's was satisfied physically, but my heart was thirsty for true love.

After our divorce, Ronnie asks me to forgive him. The truth is that I had already forgiven him before he had even asked me to. It seemed as though, the more things he did to my son and me, the more I forgave him. I didn't look down on Ronnie. I tried to encourage him to always do better. I still prayed for him. He was intelligent. He was a jack of all trades. Our pastor taught us to not love the bad things that individuals do, but to respect them as an individual. We all come short of the glory of God. I respected him as a man, but I chose not to let him back into my life to hurt me again. I also chose not to let him back into my life because he didn't want anything in life at that time. I did, I wanted life and I wanted it more abundantly. I had to go forward for myself and mostly for my son.

My sister-in-law, Helen Cox Lofton, had opened my eyes to an issue. She let me know that I had to stop being selfish because of my flesh and provide safety and love for my child. She spoke the truth in love and this truth had set me free. The truth hurts, but in due season, you'll heal. Who wants to be in a relationship that there's never any peace in? God wants us to have peace. He wants us to prosper and be in good health, even as our soul prospers. **3 John 2 "Beloved, I wish above all things that thou mayest prosper and be in health, even as thy soul prospereth."**

At times, I felt so sorry for his pain. There were so many times that he was beaten severely. He had to get stitches in his head so many times. He has had both of his jaws broken before several times. His face was beaten so many times. It was mostly because of his drug activity in the streets. Even though we were divorced, I still pray that he truly allowed Christ to come into his heart.

I had always wanted to have another child. One night I caught Ronnie talking to one of his female friends from the liquor house on the telephone. I picked up the telephone and asked who she was.

The woman assured me that she didn't want my husband. She said that she wanted me. I asked Ronnie, "Why would you let her talk to me that way, and wouldn't say anything to her." She must have wanted him, because they have a daughter together, today.

My two ex-husbands, I didn't hate them. I am not in love with them. I had never wished anything bad on them. I wanted them to succeed. I figured that if we were friends before we got married that we could be at least friends after a divorce. Our marriages didn't make it, but I wanted them to still have a wonderful life. They were beautiful people inside.

I heard that Ronnie was trying to get his life together. Even though our marriage didn't work out, he was really a comical person. He would do some of the most comical things, and you would have to laugh. I am proud of him just knowing that he was getting the help that he needed to overcome his substance abuse. Yet, unfortunately, he passed away six months after my first husband had passed away. No, I am not a black widow. I didn't kill them and I didn't collect on an insurance policy. I pray that their souls continue to rest in heaven. I had grieved for a long time before I met my third ex-husband.

TWELVE

I Am on Disability: Deliverance Shall Come

I USED TO work in Raleigh, NC at the Employee Security Commission Office in the Tax Wage Record's Department as a Data Entry Operator II. I drove from Wilson to Raleigh for almost ten months. I began noticing while I was driving that I was getting uncontrollably sleepy on the highway. One time, I woke up and I found myself riding in the grass. If I hadn't woken up, I seriously believe that I wouldn't be here today.

One time while I was diving back to Durham from Wilson, I was riding in the middle of a two lane highway going in the same direction. I remember that it was on 70 West. I had my son on the car with me. He was sleep and I had fallen asleep too. Whenever, I had awakened, I take it that the cars riding behind me were too afraid to blow their horns at me. Sometimes when you startle people, it could cause a person to have an accident.

So many times, I have fallen asleep at stop lights. People would blow their horns at me. Then I would drive further. When I came to long stoplights, standing still would make me fall asleep easily. I didn't realize that I had sleep apnea. My body kept getting more and more tired. I knew that I would sleep all night long and still felt very, very exhausted the next morning. I told the Lord, "I know that if I do not find out what is wrong, I'm going to die." I wanted to live and not die. My mom died when I was 14, and I didn't want to die and leave my son behind by him being so young. I wanted to see him grow up.

My ex-husband, Ronnie, a couple of times shook me at night and yelled, "Geneva, you just stopped breathing." I ended up mentioning that to my doctor, Dr. Nelms. Soon Dr. Nelms sent me to Dr. Lindsey de Guehery's office. I had the sleep study done and it showed that I had severe problems with sleep apnea. God kept me alive. I remember the times that my ex-husband said that I had stopped breathing, the awesome dreams that I were having. Where they really dreams, or where I really at the throne of God? I believe they weren't dreams. I believe that it was reality. I didn't see Jesus' face, but in the dreams, I was stretching out my hand to touch Him. I wasn't an adult at the throne that I was standing at. I was a little girl again. Every time that I had stretched out my hand I would wake up before I touched Jesus. I believe that if I had touched Jesus' hands I would have died. I would not be here today.

I used to be so afraid to die. Now, today, I feel that I will not go anywhere until God gets ready for me to go. God loves all of us. If God says that it's not my time to go, I will not be going anywhere until God gets ready for me to leave this earth.

I also take medicine for anxiety. I have been dealing with anxiety since 1994 and hadn't been diagnosed until about 1996. In 2005, my doctor had to adjust the anxiety medication because I was hallucinating. It was terrible. I could feel something like rats running underneath my pillow while I was sleeping. I could feel something kiss me on my lips. When I felt something kiss me on my lips, I would knock my c-pap mask off my face. Also, I could see a brown finger touch me on my face. I was pleading the blood of Jesus, though. I would get up and anoint my entire house with praying oil. I thank God that she adjusted the medication. Now, I no longer hallucinate. I take diabetes medications and I take cholesterol medications as well.

Even though I haven't gone back to work full-time, I work part-time as a Substitute Teacher. It's very rewarding to me to work for the school system. If I can help or encourage a student to be successful in life, then I know that my labor is not in vain. I try to encourage the students to get a good education and be responsible for his or herself. I tell them to get grants and scholarships so that they won't have to pay back a $190,000.00 college school loan like I have to pay back.

THIRTEEN

People That Have Influenced My Life

THERE ARE SO many people that have impacted my life. I could only put a few in my book, because I wouldn't have enough room for everybody. Some of these peoples are Marcia Wilson, the late Charlene Denise Burch, Frances Crumel Roberts, Mary Poole Cooper, Angela Denise Moore, Tyquesha Moore, and Mrs. Diane Stallings, RN. Some other people that have made an impact on my life are Johnie Ray Lofton, Dorothy McNair Lofton, the late Pastor Kenneth Lofton, Co-Pastor Helen Ann Cox Lofton, Dr. Rudolph and Windie Lofton, Frostina and Harold Renfrow. Yet, my greatest influence is Jesus Christ of Nazareth.

I remember when I was working at LabCorp that I had met a young lady by the name of **Marcia Wilson**. My self-esteem was severely low. It seemed as though every time I said what I couldn't do, she always said, "Geneva, girl, you can do it." I want to thank her for always encouraging me. I don't know whether or not she is still at LabCorp working, but I have a revelation that we must speak life to every situation. I think about Ezekiel Chapter 37. God told him to prophesy or speak to the dry bones so that they could live. If I kept on saying what I couldn't do, I probably would have never done it.

The word of God is never truer when it talks about the power of life and death is in our tongues. I believe that if we keep on speaking and believing the doubt and unbelief, we're not going to get anything from God. The word of God says that when we ask, we must ask in faith and nothing wavering.

We must also believe in ourselves. We are not to be arrogant and think of ourselves more highly than what we ought to, but we are to know that we mean a lot to God. God sent heaven's best to the earth to redeem us from sin so that we can have eternal life.

My friend, the late Charlene Denise Burch let me stay with her in Durham, NC, whenever I had no other place to go. She had four children and I was there with her at Chapel Hill whenever her twins were born. Charlene and I had met at Kittrell Job Corps. We really had enjoyed being at Kittrell. Charlene and I used to enjoy going to the dances there almost every Friday night. She had really been an inspiration to me. She was very short. She was pleasantly fluffy, but she carried her weight very well. She always looked very nice everywhere she went. That goes to show, anybody given the right clothes, perfumes, colognes, or a little bit of make-up, can look so nice. We really know that real beauty comes from within. I thank God for her encouraging me. She was the kind of person that always told me the truth with love. She had never raised her voice whenever she was telling me the truth. I know that wisdom was always spoken from her lips. Even though we had lost contact with one another for a moment, we had reconnected. I miss her after she went on to be with the Lord. She died the same year that Covid 19 rushed upon our earth.

I give a very loud shout out to my niece, **Frances Crumel Roberts**. She relocated to Atlanta, GA. We grew up together.

Although she is one year older than I am, she sometimes tells other people that I am her cousin, instead of her aunt. I used to love it whenever Frances would come visit us. She has always had a love for animals. She liked for me to take her down to the hog pin. Frances would take a long stick and scratch the hog's back. She loved all kinds of animals. I used to like going to spend the night with her in Middlesex, North Carolina, while we were growing up together. Sometimes whenever she didn't want to share her toys with me, she would splash soap in my eyes while we were in the bathtub. She didn't mine fighting every once in a while. She's been through so much, but we are like sisters instead of me being her aunt. She is married to a great man of God, Irvin Roberts and she has an intelligent, beautiful daughter called Rachel Kelly Martin.

I honor my second ex-husband's sister, Mary Poole Cooper. Sometimes whenever husbands and wives get divorces the ex-wife or ex-husband doesn't have much to do with the divorced family. I just truly thank God for my ex-husband's sister. I look at the ways that she had really struggled to fight for her family. At one time in Mary's life she had struggled with substance abuse. She used to drink a little, but her greatest struggle was crack, cocaine.

I had at one time seen how the substance abuse took hold of her life and wanted to destroy her. A couple of years ago, the crack, cocaine almost made her loose her mind. We don't know until this day, whether or not somebody had put something extra in the drugs. It took a couple of weeks for her to leave the house. She had refused to go to get help at the clinic, but she did make up in her mind to stop using drugs. She sincerely cried out unto God and asked Him for help. I believe that whether through a treatment center or whether through being in the face of God, if an individual wants to be set free from substance abuse, he or she will. I also believe that this statement is true whether it is about substance abuse, hatred, lust, strife, and about all sin in general. I believe when a person really gets sick and tired of what he or she is doing; a change for the best will come.

I am so glad she didn't give up. Today, I am so proud of my sister-in-law. Whenever she was living in Stantonsburg, North Carolina she still allowed me to come and get my nieces and nephews for church. She has never stopped being kind to me, and that has been since the first day that we've ever met. At several times, we wouldn't have eaten if it weren't for her. I remember times when her brother, Ronnie, my ex-husband, had messed up our food money. She had given us some food to eat. She's an amazing cook. She's very kind to all that she meets, and she loves her children and her grandchildren. I really like the way that she dresses. She has inspired me not to be so conservative. I need to dress my age and not like I am a hundred year old woman. I want Mary Poole Cooper to know that she inspired me. I am very proud of her. I would like to see her get married to the love of her life.

Shortly after, I came out of the mental hospital; I knew that I didn't even have the strength to go back to work. I thank God for my friend and cousin **Angela D. Moore**. I was going through my separation and a divorce, but my friend let my son and me stay with her for a couple of months. I love her and her daughter, **Tyquesha Ford-Moore**. I was so anxious and sick. I was broken down in my body and my mind. I felt like I could never smile again. I was sick mentally, physically, economically, emotionally, and financially. I had a mental breakdown April 2004. I was at Wilson Medical and was transferred to Wayne Memorial's mental ward.

Some people when they are stressed respond differently. Whenever I got stressed out, my body would get very weak. Stress would paralyze me and leave me with only a little energy. I couldn't even focus on how to drive my car. I would cry for hours. I would cry because I was crying and half the time I didn't even know why. Yet, I believe sometimes I was crying because I felt that I had failed in life itself. My focus was way off. I let the troubles of life get me down. I asked the doctor to check my brain and make sure all my brain cells weren't dead. I felt helpless and hopeless. My God allowed me to have hope again. Without God's Spirit and His word, I would have been gone on to glory. My friends and family, Angie and Tyquesha helped to nurse me back to health again. I didn't say that every day was peaches and cream. We would fuss sometimes, but I still respected her and her child.

I believe that whenever you are a guest in somebody else's home, you need not to treat it like it's your own. If they invite you in, keep their place extra clean. Even if they say not to worry about doing so, keep it extra clean anyhow. Cleanliness is not the only thing to do whenever you live with someone else. If you can, help them financially as well. If you can give, give. Do not let them take advantage of you, but help as much as you can. I believe that we as Christian sisters were a blessing to one another.

My brother, Kenneth, called us Laverne and Shirley. We do not always agree on everything, but by us being cousins, friends, and sisters in Christ Jesus, we grew stronger as friends. We use to pray together almost every day. Angie is a very nice woman of God. I always hoped that her Boaz finds her. He did find her. She is surely a praying woman, and she loves God with all of her heart. Her daughter Tyquesha is very precious. She really makes my day with her kindness and love. I will always love them. Thank you Angela and Tyquesha for all that you have done and continue to do in my life. May God bless the two of you for your help in raising Anthony and Elijah Stiles.

I remember that I was in the Work Study Program at Wilson Community College in Wilson, North Carolina. I was working for **Mrs. Diane Stalling the R.N**. Mrs. Diane Stallings is a one of a kind lady. I loved **Mrs. Diane, Mrs. Corlis, and Mrs. Lisa** as well. They were always encouraging me. I want to give special thanks to **Mr. Franky**, Mrs. Diane's husband.

Mr. Franky would send me sandwiches by his wife. Nobody knew how bad financially my son and I were going through. Many of times the sandwiches that were made for me and the homemade soup that was made by Mrs. Diane was a ram in the bush whenever my food got a little low. God has always made a way for us. God has never let us down. If I was in need and didn't get it, it was because I didn't ask God for it. There were times in my life whenever He just brought finances to me right out of the blue. God has always been there for me. He has always been right on time, every time that I had needed a helping hand.

I thank God for my older brother, **Johnie Ray Lofton**. He's been through times of substance abuse, but he came back to the Lord. Johnie and his wife, **Dorothy McNair Lofton**, are serving God in our church faithfully until this day. They are truly soul winners. They used to go out and bring people to the house of the Lord. What is extra ordinary about him is the fact that he doesn't even know how to read, but he reaches the world with the gospel. I want to share with you the crucial experience that completely turned his life around.

Brother Johnie kept being in and out of church. The saints kept praying that He would come back to God. On one in 2007 after a day of him getting high with his friends, he encountered hell. He had an outer body experience where God allowed him to experience hell itself. Brother Johnie's wife had talked to him about going back to church. He told her that he wasn't going back to church anymore. She told him that she was going to bed. He told her to go ahead because he wasn't going right that moment. At around 11:00 pm, Johnie put his pajamas on. He went to bed. No later than he closed his eyes and opened them back up, he appeared in hell. He began to see darkness. Then he could see people standing in round holes with saliva like a hot volcano. He could see people inside screaming and yelling. They wanted help. He was frightened. He realized that he was down there. He kept calling on the Lord. He called on God and a voice told him to come on the other side. He began to walk and he came to a big mansion like a castle. When he got to the castle, the gates opened up. A man was standing there in a white robe. The white robe was so white that it looked like the sun shining. The man's hair was cold dark black and it was long. He began to ask the man how he can get back to the other side because he wanted to get out of there. The man's voice didn't sound like ours. The man told him to go back with praise in his heart. Everything began to go back down. He appeared back in his body like an earthquake was dropping. He was singing a worship song. Whenever he came back through his clothes were soaking wet. His feet were burning and the skin had wrinkled up on his feet. That's how extremely hot it was. He got up Sunday morning and told his wife about it. He went to church. He told his testimony at church. Ever since that day he has never stopped being dedicated to God. I am so proud of him. I know that he is telling the truth because, my brother Johnie Lofton, doesn't even know how to read. Some of the things that he has described are in the book called "Revelation to Hell."

I've had so many people that came into my life, but the ones that have made the greatest impact on my spiritual life are the **late Pastor Kenneth Lee Lofton** and his wife **Co-Pastor Helen Ann**

Cox Lofton. Whenever I was about 13 years old, before mom died, I gave my life to Jesus Christ at **Trinity Deliverance Center**. It is still located at 408 East Vance Street here in the city of Wilson, North Carolina. The **late Pastor Carrie P. Jacobs** was the pastor and the **late Overseer Robert Jacob** was by her side. Even though pastor and overseer are gone on to be with the Lord, **Pastor Carolyn Brown** remains the pastor at Trinity Deliverance Center.

Trinity Deliverance Church is where my firm foundation began. The word of God is right. I had strayed away from God but what I had learned as a child in church brought me back to God. Whenever my brother came back to Wilson from being in the army a couple of years, our dad, Willie James Lofton, had died in 1996. In 1997, I moved back to Wilson County and stayed with my brother again and his wife. They had already begun what is now Solid Rock Ministries. My brother, which was also my pastor, preached and taught the word of God. By them living a holy lifestyle and teaching the word of God, they have caused my life to turn around. I didn't say that every day was perfect or that we never have disagreements. If I ever want a straight forward answer though, I can count on my sister-in-law, my Co-Pastor Helen Lofton, to tell me the truth. The truth sometimes hurt, but when given from a sincere woman or man or God, it will set you free. My pastor didn't sugar coat the word of God. He preached and taught the word the way that the Holy Spirit gave it to him. He told us that he has to tell us like God would have us to know it, because he was an under shepherd over our souls. He didn't want to miss heaven for not telling us the truth.

I thank God for the rock! Solid Rock is located at 502 SW Jordan Street here in Wilson, North Carolina at the Total Impact Outreach's church. I know that the rock is Jesus. I still have trials and tribulations. Nevertheless, God deliver me and take me through all of them. I also thank them for taking time out with my son and grandson, Timothy and Tyrran Manning. They have been a blessing to us at times whenever we were in desperate need. They are always encouraging us. I loved the late Pastor Kenneth Lofton and I love our Co-Pastor Helen Lofton that is still in charge at Solid Rock Ministries.

I thank God for my brother and my sister-in-law, **Pastor Rudolph Lofton** and **Minister Windie Locus Lofton**. They have inspired me to want to do something for myself. They work so hard. They have public jobs, but they also used to go down and work at their clothing store. The name of the store was **Windie's Boutique**. She was located on Tarboro Street downtown in the City of Wilson, but she doesn't have the downtown shop anymore.

Sometimes we keep calling out for God to bless us. I've learned that God will bless the work of our hands. I am writing this book and I will be doing a gospel CD so that God can bless the work of my hands. I give my tithes and my offering according to Malachi the third chapter. I want all what god has for me. I do not only want to give God the financial part, I want to give Him my life, my praise and worship, time, and anything else that He asks me for. I've never seen the righteous forsaken. Have you? **Psalm 37:4 "Delight thyself also in the LORD; And he shall give thee the desires of thine heart."**

I thank God for my sister and her husband, **Frostina Lofton Renfrow** and **Harold Renfrow.** They took me in whenever I was 16 years old. I was a little disobedient at times, but I thank God for them. They were very patient with me. They gave support to me. I admired the knowledge that my brother-in-law, Harold possesses. He's so intelligent. He takes care of his family. He knows how to take care of his finances. I thank them for having a hand in raising me, and also for their help in watching over my son, Timothy. I appreciate my sister, Frostina for always encouraging me. I can talk to my sister about anything. I've never hear anything that I tell her in secret be told to anybody else. Frostina is truly a woman of God. I love her, she is my angel. I pray that God blesses them to have children of their own someday. She helped me get my divorce from my third husband. I would have written it up myself, but I had to get a lawyer from Dominican Republic to act on my behalf. Her name is Jacqueline Tavarez. She represented me in Dominican Republic, but I first had to go to Washington, D.C. in order to get the paperwork for her to represent me because I got married in Dominican Republic.

I thank God for Francisco Alatorre in Alsip, Illinois. Even though we didn't always agree on the word of God, we encouraged one another in the Lord. Even though there are so many denominations in the world today, we as the people of God have to come together, put aside our traditions and just tell the good news. We all know that the good news is about Jesus. Jesus, came, died, and rose again to set us all free from the bondage of sin and lead us back into the presence of the Most High God.

I thank God for my friend and neighbor, **Margaret Ruth Green**. She lives on the other side of the street from me. Whenever we are together, we laugh and have an awesome time together. She is another one that likes to speak her peace. Even though she is almost 79 years old, she dresses younger and sassy. She encourages me a lot whenever I go through the turmoil in life, and she told me to stop talking to the crazy, scammers online. I am fine by myself until God sends me a husband. Her son, **Keyshone Boose** is my godson.

My greatest influence was Jesus. He has saved my soul. Jesus has set me free from the bondage of sin, shame, defeat, and from eternal damnation. I know that without Jesus Christ of Nazareth being in my life, I am destined for destruction and in hell I will lift up my eyes. Thank you, sweet Jesus for being the God of my salvation. I love you Jesus for evermore because you first loved me.

FOURTEEN

I Am Free to Be Me

WHY DO PEOPLE look at me as being a grandma, I do not know. I am only about two years older than my cousin and friend **Angela D. Moore**. People always think that I am her mom, and they think that I am her daughter's grandma. Yet, her daughter, **Tyquesha Ford-Moore** is my goddaughter.

I try to dress as young as I can, but most of the time, much older men look at me. I asked the Lord, "Jesus why do people think that I am so old?" I am really up for suggestions. Most of the times, it doesn't bother me. Every now and then, whenever I want to have a pity party for myself, it bothers me. I believe that I need a makeover. First of all, I believe I need a makeover inwardly. Maybe I'm not as confident about myself like I need to be because I've been crushed about my looks in the past. Lord Jesus, please make me over again. **Psalm 139:14 "I will praise thee; for I am fearfully and wonderfully made: marvelous are thy works; and that my soul knoweth right well."**

For years and years, I believed that I was trying to be someone else. I looked at other people lives and I wanted to be like others. It's not wrong to model oneself after someone that is holy, positive, mature, and productive. Yet, each and every one has an assignment from God that is unique. I had wanted to look like Halle Berry. I do not have the body frame to be her, and I don't have her face or her hair.

One day our pastor was talking and he was just telling us to be who we are in Christ Jesus. He said we need to know who God called us to be and be that. Sometimes people in other positions look better. We all are important in the body of Christ Jesus. We need to all work together as one. We do not need to be jealous of each other. We need to all work with one another to get this gospel out to those that do not know Jesus Christ as their personal Savior.

I thank God that I know that I am someone great in Christ Jesus. Whenever I was going to school, I used to be picked on almost every day. Most of the time the first thing people would notice was my ears. My ears stick out. Sometimes the kids called me Dumbo. Now in today's society, I get picked on because my butt doesn't stick out like other women butts do. Well, sometimes it bothers me, but most of the time, I have to realize that God didn't give me a big butt like other women. Some women might desire to have beautiful girls up top like I do.

We as individuals need to take what the good Lord has given us and work with it. We can't allow television to always dictate to us what and who is beautiful. Beauty is really skin deep. We can take some of the most beautiful people in the world, and he or she can be so cruel and have a nasty attitude within. We can also take some of the most humble and not so beautiful people in society, and they have a pure, kind, and loving heart.

I can only be me. As long as I do the will of my Father which arts in Heaven, I believe that is the best beauty that I can offer. I want most of the beauty to come from within. I believe that being beautiful inside causes an individual to want to be beautiful out-wardly. You'll be surprised what a beautiful woman and a handsome man can become whenever she or he is loved and nurtured by the right individual and especially when that individual is nurtured by God Almighty. God can clean up the sinner and that individual may become unrecognizable whenever he or she allows God to turn a situation around in his or her life.

Now, I am free to be me. I don't have to be anybody else, because I will fail every time trying to be someone else. I can only be me, a child of the King Jesus, and be free. He who Christ has set free is surely free indeed. **John 8:36 "If the Son therefore shall make you free, ye shall be free indeed."**

FIFTEEN

The Craziest Things I've Done

I'VE DONE SOME of the craziest things in my life like zipping my lips up in my coat jacket, and burning my lips with a hot curling iron. I've also had incidents with Clorox, my skirt, fried chicken, strawberry cake, my hair, and with my eyebrows.

I remember one day whenever I was at Kittrell Job Corps, I had zipped my lips up in my coat zipper by mistake. I had my head bent down while I was zipping up my coat really fast. Ooooops, I zipped my coat up extremely too fast. My lips had gotten caught in my coat's zipper. You can imagine the terrible pain.

I took up Cosmetology at Vance Granville Community College in Henderson, NC while I was at Kittrell Job Corps. I was getting ready to do somebody's hair in the dorm. I wanted to make sure that the curlers were hot. I do not know what possessed me to see if I could smell how hot the curlers were. I had the professional kind, and it had a long flap on it whenever it was opened. That flap on the curlers flew backwards and smacked me on my lips. I had the imprint of the curlers on both my top and bottom lips. It was crucial pain. That was surely one of the hottest kisses that I've ever had!

One day when I was living with my sister, Frostina, I made a mistake and turned over a Clorox jug whenever we came back from doing our laundry. The lid must not have been screwed on very tight. My God, they had light, mint green carpet. Could you imagine the big stain left from the Clorox? I was so afraid. My sister kept saying, "Geneva, do you smell Clorox in your room." I said, "No, I do not." I was shaking in my boots. After a little while, she moved my clothes basket around and she had found that Clorox spot underneath it. She said, "Now, granny, why in this world did you try to hide that Clorox spot?" Years later, we still laugh about the Clorox spill.

You would have thought that I had enough issues with Clorox. One day, I had spilled red Kool-Aid in the living room. This was the same apartment with this light, mint green carpet. I tried dish detergent. I said, "I've got to get these stains up. I'll just use a little Clorox." Ummmm, it made things worst. Just imagine how mint green carpet looks with bright yellow stains on it. I was still, yet afraid to tell my sister. I can't even remember how mad they were. They must have put me in a category with Denace the Menace. Occasionally, we still laugh about it till this day.

I remember one time whenever I went to sing in a club in downtown Durham, NC. I had gone to the bathroom while I was there. I went back to the table where my sister, Frostina and my sister-in-law Dee were sitting. I went to ask the man when I was going to perform my song. I kept wondering why people were staring at me constantly. Whenever I got back to my seat, my sister said, "Granny, your skirt in the back is jacked up in your stockings. I was so embarrassed! She said whenever I stepped away from the table that she tried to pull it down, but I moved so fast that she couldn't pull it down for me.

I've had crazy stuff to happen to me, but none was crazier than whenever I lost my skirt in public. I wanted to say that the place is called Kangaroo now on 64 Highway in Wilson, North Carolina. I believe it used to be called Bullets when this occurred. I do remember it was on Mother's Day. We were riding in my sister-in-law's van. We were all going after church to go see my brother that was at the VA Hospital in Durham, North Carolina. I had just gone in to the store to get some hot dogs. I had no idea that my skirt had come loose. I felt a draft. I had a bag in one hand. In that same hand, I held Timothy, my son's hand. In the other hand, I held my nephew's hand, Patrick Horne. Oooops, I started feeling too much of a breeze. I looked down and my skirt was on the payment. I was standing there in broad daylight in my blouse and my panty hoses. I didn't even have on a slip that day. I tried to hand my son and nephew my bag, but they were pointing at me and laughing. I pulled my skirt up and rushed to open the van door, and I almost lost the skirt again. My nephew and my son laughed me down that day. One of the ministers named Lillian said, "Sister Geneva, why are you trying to show your tail on Mother's Day?" We laughed and laughed. There were cars that were pulling up to the gas station. I guess that the men that were with their spouses were too afraid to stare at me.

I remember one time, when I first began to cook at my sister house, how I wanted to surprise them and have supper ready for them whenever they got home. Oh, my God. It was my first time frying some good old southern fried chicken. The chicken was so beautifully, brown on the outside and just as bloody on the inside! How embarrassing was that?

One time I baked my sister, Frostina's birthday cake. I didn't know that I was supposed to only put one can of frosting on a cake, but I used two cans of frosting on it. That strawberry cake was some kind of rich; nevertheless, we ate every last bit of it.

My sister says to never leave me home on a rainy day. I used to have a jerry curl in my hair. Well, one rainy day, I wanted to try something new. I went to the store and got me an S-Curl. S-Curls are basically for people with short hair. It will make very short hair look curly. My hair was long. By the time I had finished putting that S-Curl into my hair, my hair was completely straight before my sister got home from work. She asked me what was going on. I had no good answer for her. I was fresh out of Cosmetology school and thought that I was very professional.

I do not know what possessed me to do this, but whenever I had first met my second husband, I wanted to look nice. I went out and got me a box perm. I wanted my eyebrows to look slick too. I had rubbed some of the perm on my eyebrows. I had burned the tender part up under my eyebrows. People look at my eyebrows and think that I have on dark makeup, but that darkness came from me putting that perm on my eyebrows, and the perm burned me.

So now you know how a rainy day can make a person act like Dennis the Menace? Think about some of the craziest things you have done. Come on now. I know that you want to laugh too.

SIXTEEN

Can I Rely On Internet Dating?

I AM A child of God, for heaven's sake. I need to be patient and wait on God for my husband. I felt like Sarah and Abraham. Sarah wanted to have a child so bad that she didn't want to wait on the Lord for the promised child. She was going to help the Lord out. So Sarah allowed Abraham to have a child by her Egyptian handmaiden, Hagar. God ended up telling Abraham that Ishmael wasn't the promise, but Isaac was the promised child that he had to wait for. It's the same way with my dating life. Even though I have heard of some successful marriages that started from Internet Online Dating, the internet wasn't the way for me to find love. I needed to wait on God to meet someone in person.

Well, I thought I would give the Christian websites a try so that I could find someone to talk to an Ishmael. Maybe, I was trying to help God out like Sarah did. I was getting a little lonely you know. I needed to have waited on God for that husband, an Isaac.

I've found myself on three websites. I was talking to different people. Most of the people were up there for money only. After they knew that I wasn't going to give them anything, they had stopped talking to me. One person that I gave a gift card to played mind games. He only would give you his undivided attention whenever he was getting something from you. He was playing me and this other girl at the same time, and she texted me and told me that she found out that he wasn't really in the army. A lot of the scammers pretend that he is in the army on a mission in another country so that he doesn't have to show his face on the camera.

I've met some wonderful individual online though. Some of the nice ones are Francisco Alatorre John B, Chad, Kevin C, Kevin L. and Rexford Bio from Ghana, but the one I truly thought about was Franky Luciano. I couldn't fall deep, because there wasn't anyone to catch me but God. I found out that this Franky Luciano wasn't who he said that he was. We used to chat almost every day. We had talked on the telephone a couple of times.

I have been warned that online dating can't be trusted. Believe it or not, I'm still yet praying. I know that people have gotten married by internet dating, but I am trying to use common sense, because I can't really see the person that is truly on the other side of a computer. Recently, I had chatted with a young man online. His picture was a white man's picture. He finally broke down and he told me that he was a black man and he wasn't even from where he said that he had lived.

Due to that incident, I've made up in my mine to wait on God for my Boaz. I am going to wait by doing the work of the ministry. I'll be praying, studying, and seeking the face of God. That way I will not allow myself to get caught up in emotions. I will look at reality. I will never get married again until God has assured me that he is the right one. I refuse to mess up another man's life or allow him to mess up my life, nor my son's or grandson's life.

I am human, and by me having sexual relationships in the past, my box gets hot sometimes. I try not to look at movies showing a lot of erotic things on them. I can make it because I haven't heard of anyone dying because of lack of sex. At least this is what our pastor says. God has been keeping me from performing any sexual activities. It's because I want to be kept, and I do not put myself in places that could lead to fornication. It's a choice that each and every individual has to make for him or herself.

Scammers have new tricks now. Some of them are using videos to make you think that you're chatting with them. You may think that you're chatting with someone famous because you see the person talking on the chat. Yet, try asking the person questions while on video chat and see if they can answer questions and have a conversation with you. Most of the time, that scammer will hang up because he or she is just playing a famous person's video or taking the famous person's video and putting on his or her profile. Don't deposit any checks from anyone. Don't allow people to send any codes to your telephone. He or she will ask you for that code and take over your identity.

I trusted too many people online. The buck stops here with me using wisdom. I gave money to someone that said that he wanted to come visit me. He took the money and claimed that he had to spend it on his mom's hospital bill and then he had to spend money on her funeral. Save your money and take yourself and your kids out to dinner, buy a new wig, get your feet done, and etc. I don't know about anyone else, but whenever an individual works as hard as most of the American people do in our country, we don't have time to be scammed out of our money. We don't need for our money to be used on other people so that they can enjoy their lives at our expense. Let's wise up this year. We need to really pray to God for a spouse and not allow scammers to continue to abuse us as children of God. The scammers try to make you feel ashamed because you are a Christian, and they expect Christians to always be helpful. We are Christians, but we don't have to be a fool for anyone. The scammers need to watch very careful how he or she handles a child of God. **Matthew 18:6 "But whoso shall offend one of these little ones which believe in me, it were better for him that a millstone were hanged about his neck, and that he were drowned in the depth of the sea."**

I am not God, but I can honestly give some good advice about internet dating from my own experience. Please be careful. I've ran into a lot of people that ask for money. They have some stories to tell you. They had some that I haven't even heard from my ex-husbands. I believe in friendship online. Nevertheless, I am going to have to wait on God right now, because I've seen the crooked ones online outweigh the good ones.

SEVENTEEN

Online Dating Again: I Had Dismissed the Warning Signs

YOU KNOW WHENEVER a child of God is disobedient, God allows that child to be chastised. I should have took my own advice and left the online activity alone all together. Whenever I went back online, I really lost a lot whenever it came to relationships. I was disobedient to God. Scammers are very professional online. Some of them don't always directly ask you for money all the time. At times he will tell you situations that are going on in his life that he needs money for. The scammer wants you to suggest that you will help them to pay money towards the problems that he needs fixing. After a while, he will make you feel as if you're the bad person for not helping.

I was in some online relationships that cost me all together about 5,000 dollars. Yet, this last marriage which came from online, the pen pal site, which was my third marriage cost me about $25,000.00. He came from Dominican Republic and it took a little over three years for him to get his visa and green card in order to come to America. I was on a pen pal sight. I can't even remember which one it was. In

October or late September, 2018, I met my last husband. I was saying to myself, "who is this Mexican man calling me?" He quickly cleared it up by telling me that he wasn't Mexican but Dominican.

He quickly started calling me from his job and from his house. He began introducing me by telephone to his co-workers, family, and his friends. About 2 weeks later he had asked me to marry him. I should had said no because it was too fast to fall in love. I hadn't had any sexual contact in seven years before I met him. We had planned to get married during the Christmas holiday of 2018, but one of my papers had expired and I had to pay the lawyer in Dominican Republic in order to get different paperwork. Therefore, we got married January, 2019.

As a wife, the only thing that I wanted to do was to be loved and know that my husband was truly in love with me. That's really what most of our heated discussions were really about finances, honor, true love, and helping to provide for me. I sinned against God as a spiritual leader. I had confessed that I had slept with this man before marriage, whenever I went to see him in Dominican Republic. That was my first mistake because I knew better as a leader, and I was very aware of God's word. '

I really loved my ex-husband, Alberto. I helped him get a car that I paid for two and half years until he came to America. Sometimes, I even sent money to pay for his tires on the vehicle and gas to put in the car. I was skeptical at first, because for some reason he had to get the car put in his cousin's name. I was very angry, but I knew that he needed a vehicle. My sister said that if you got to go so far as to send some gas money from another country, he needs to sell the car. She told me to stop being for a fool and wise up.

I have learned that a man or a woman needs to stay single if he or she or both are stuck in his or her ways and doesn't ever want to change. A marriage is about pleasing each other. It's not about only one person having his or her way all the time. Also, children are a beautiful thing to have in a marriage. Yet, there is an order of relationship in a marriage. God should come first, then the spouse, and then the children. If that spouse is a good spouse and he or she is not abusing the relationship with the spouse or children, the children don't need to be first in that married couple's life. I remembered whenever my ex-husband from Dominican Republic told me that God came first, then his children, then his mom, and then me. Sometimes while in Dominican Republic, he wanted me to sit in the back seat of the car whenever his daughter wanted to sit in the front seat.

One time I went to Dominican Republic after the pandemic was cooling down in March 2021. My ex-husband took me to some type of motel that we could only stay at for three hours. After making love, right out of the blue, he said, I understand if you want a divorce. I wondered where did this come from, him talking like that. The next thing that I know about two days later he took me to a woman's house. He said that he was going to see his goddaughter. I didn't know that he had even had a goddaughter. Her mom is very beautiful and single, and I've seen her and her daughter ride in our car before, while I was talking to him on the telephone. Two evenings in a row, my ex would sit at his mom's kitchen table to stare at his goddaughter mom's picture. He would even let his cousins see the picture to verify that she was beautiful. I would lie down in the bed and cry my eyeballs out. No man should keep starring and bragging about how beautiful another woman was that much. He said that they were just friends, but my heart told me something different. I regret crying so much because the crying was getting on my mother-in-law's nerves. Please forgive me. He even went outside and called his daughter. While talking on the telephone he told his cousins to look at "Diablo", which meant devil in Spanish, because I was crying.

One time my mother-in-law was sick and she was riding in the front seat, and I had ridden in the back seat. My ex went to see a lawyer about getting some legal advice to help his mom. He told the lawyer who his mom was and what he needed help with, but fail to introduce me at all. The lawyer got inside our car and talked to his mom for about 15–20 minutes and never looked back to neither acknowledge me nor say hello. I was so upset so much that my ex stopped the car and told me to get out! I got out at the store and there were police officers there. So I asked them if they had any place that I could use the telephone to call my family back in the USA. I was jealous because he failed to introduce me at all. Even whenever he came to America, I became even more upset. He had a habit of saying that his youngest daughter's mom was his esposa when he used to pay bills for her by telephone. The reason how I knew that he was talking about her and not me was whenever he would say, "mi esposa y nina." I knew that we didn't have a daughter together; therefore, I was very offended every time that he said phrases like that. Even my sister-in-law told him to stop saying that. My sister-in-law, Helen could speak Spanish more fluently than what I could.

I remembered a time whenever I rode in the back seat with my ex's daughter and when he stopped at the corner, other people were asking for another woman that they were used to seeing him ride with. He said that the woman and he were just friends. He used to coach a girls baseball team. Whenever I arrived at the game, a young player on the opposite team told him that I weren't the same woman that he had brought before. I knew right then that he was cheating on me. Later on at the same game, one of the female ball players was injured. They said that she had problems with her heart. They gave her a chair to sit in, but she refused to sit in it. She wanted to lay her head in my ex's chest for about 30 minutes with his arms wrapped around her. Whenever, I addressed the situation, he cursed me out in front of everyone. Whenever the ambulance got there they didn't put her in it. Therefore, I know that laying her head in his chest with his arms wrapped around her was her kind of way as exposing their relationship together.

There was a lot of money that had been spent during this Dominican Republic marriage. I really tried to help support my ex until he was able to come to the United States. I sent money every month to assist him until he found a good paying job here in the United States after his green card was approved. Now, he would work faithfully unless he was sick. He made about $22.00 an hour, but he sent 90% of his money to Dominican Republic. He had always told me that I would never be first in his life whenever he came to the US. He mentioned that I would never change his ways. Therefore, I decided to change my way and divorce him. I am not a footstool for a man. I am a queen and a daughter of the Most High God.

My ex and I used to make love until we got tired. Whenever we had our own apartment in Puerto Plata in Dominican Republic, he used to cook for me or bring me home something to eat every day from work. Even though at times, he used to ask me for lots money, we still had a good relationship. I like the times whenever he would say, "Get dressed and put on something nice." He would take me to Ocean World to eat pizza. Ocean World in Puerto Plata has the best pizza. One time I won first place whenever I sang a song at Ocean World. They gave me a free pass to use for one day, but I didn't get a chance to use it.

I had visited Dominican Republic six times and stayed months at a time. Even whenever my ex and I stayed at his mom's house, we were still close, even though we used to fuss. Yet, whenever he came to the United States, I had to beg for his affection. He used to greet me with kisses in Dominican, but whenever he came to the USA, he said that he didn't do a lot of kissing. I began to realize that my ex's heart was no longer mine anymore. He talked more on the telephone to his Spanish speaking family and friends than he did with me. He told my sister-in-law that the reason why he didn't talk that much with me is because I didn't speak a lot of Spanish. He knew that I didn't speak a lot of Spanish whenever we met me, but love and affection can still be shown in a marriage through any type of language barrier.

At times he would be speaking so sweet and tender to other women. Whenever he first came to America, I woke up from sleeping and heard him talking to a female. He told the lady that I was his esposa, but she was his love. She needed to have hope in him. At times, I used to get so mad at him because I would ask who he was talking to and he would hang up the telephone. Then he would switch and call someone else and say that the second person that he called was the first person that he originally was talking to. He would wait until the times that I was upset to call people for me to talk to whenever I was upset. It was like he wanted people to always see me at my worst state to cover up the times that I would catch him talking to other women. He guarded his telephone like a watch dog, and always took it with him wherever he went, even to the shower.

One time whenever I was over in Dominican Republic in 2021, he sat in my lap. His daughter's brother kept saying the word Puerto Rican a couple of times. The next time I heard him say Puerto Rican is when he was talking to one of his friends about how the Puerto Rican was a muneca. I heard it again whenever his friend said Puerto Rica at the table while we were eating. My ex would wait until we are out in public to show me up because he knew that I would get mad about other women that he claims that he wasn't involved with. Even when in Dominican Republic, his daughter said that her daddy has a "novia" which means girlfriend. He tried to clear it up by saying my name, but his daughter said, "No." She wasn't talking about me. She was talking about another woman. There is one thing about kids. They will tell the truth most of the time. I cried and cried that evening. No matter how much my ex tried to clear things up that thought always stuck in the back of my mind. One time I had checked my ex-husband's telephone messages over in Dominican Republic. He had told his daughter's mother how he was jealous over her. I had to use my telephone to translate the messages into English. I said to myself that if he was so jealous, why they didn't get married. Yet, I have found out that they got married in 2024. He could have kept me out of the picture and saved the pain and hurt that I have gone through. To me, he wasn't a forgiving man. After we had arguments it would provoke him to talk to other women. He had texted one lady, and her last name was Rodrigues. He told her that she was always beautiful and asked her if she wanted his number. They exchanged numbers. The telephone number that was given to her was a number to a telephone that I had just purchased for him.

I had remembered one time that my family came over to our house whenever we were arguing. He called the police on us because I wanted to check his telephone messages. He felt threaten, even though nobody had threaten him at all. While the officers were outside, my niece and I saw him erase his messages. Then, in front of the police he said that it was okay to check his telephone, and he had no problems with it. I told him that I don't need to check it now, because my niece and I just saw you erase messages inside the house right in front of us before you went back out to talk with the officers. There was still an incident that put the icing on top of the cake.

I was jealous over the fact that my ex chose faithfully to call a woman on his job at his break time. I never knew her name, but he always called her Americana. Also, whenever I was at my sister's house in Wendell, he told Americana that I was there with him and he wasn't at work. Whenever he stayed out with Covid 19, he talked with Americana and told her the reason why he hadn't called her is because he was out with Covid 19 a couple of days and hadn't been to work. I immediately asked that he needs to put her on the telephone. He doesn't even call me from work like that so why is he calling her. We need to all be friends together because the relationship wasn't right. Our relationship really went farther down because I told him to put the "bi**h" on the telephone because she needs to know that you're married. Ever since then, he would stick up his middle finger and say "mothers fuck you" a lot. He also use to pull down his underwear and tell me to "kiss his a**." Even the night that I won Wilson Idol, he cursed for two hours because he was drinking. A couple of days later I walked in on him telling someone that he would buy a plane ticket for the person. That was my last draw. I knew that it was for a female because whenever I confronted him, he had a smirk on his face. He had a certain smirk on his face whenever he has been caught doing something that he has no business doing. About that time his daughter calls. I was still confronting him about the ticket. I was so mad that I was turning over the kitchen chairs because I felt like I wanted to smack him as if I was a man. I knew that right then, we didn't need to be together, because I couldn't trust him anymore. I had called the police to remove him from the home. The police told us that it was his home and cars as well and that they couldn't make him leave the house. One day, he made me so mad whenever I was washing dishes that I threw a plate on the floor and it shattered. I meant to throw it because to me that shattered plate meant that our marriage was over.

I was just humiliated. Sex was controlled and it was only whenever he desired it. I couldn't approach him sexually. If I even tried to touch him or kiss him, he would slap my hands away and tell me to leave him alone. Sex was only to satisfy his physical needs and only whenever he just had to sleep with me. I couldn't hug nor kiss him and I only had sex whenever he was ready about once time a week or twice a week if I was lucky. I felt as though he had found a girlfriend either at Smithfield Packing Company here in Wilson, North Carolina or at Wilson Tech where he was studying English at night.

I felt like he was saving himself sexually for the person that he truly loved. Trust me, a woman knows whenever a man really loves her or just tolerates her. I could often hear bit and pieces of his conversation. He used to tell people that I cooked and cleaned, but we didn't sleep together. That means that I cooked and clean for him, but he wasn't sleeping with me. It was half true. He slept with me sexually, but it wasn't all the time.

EIGHTEEN

Divorce, It's Like A Death

WHAT PEOPLE SOMETIMES do not realize is that a divorce feels like a death. I do believe that sometimes it's more devastating to the relatives that come into your life than the couples themselves. I believe that if it weren't for love of my ex-husband's relatives that we would have broken up a long time before we got our divorce.

I have learned so much about being a wife three times. My pastors, the late Kenneth Lofton and Co-Pastor Helen Lofton, taught the congregation well. I never, ever again would like to have a broken marriage. I want God to be the center of my joy. I want to honor my husband and be a woman of virtue just like the Word of God tells me to be in **Proverbs the 31st Chapter**. I believe that God is preparing me this time for marriage because He knows that I really desire to be with someone that loves me for me and not for what they can get out of me. I want a spouse than can lead me into the presence of God, and we can do ministry in God's vineyard together. One of my main problems was that I allowed husbands to come into my life and we weren't going in the same directions. **II Corinthians 6:14 "Be ye not unequally yoked together with unbelievers: for**

what fellowship hath righteousness with unrighteousness? And what communion hath light with darkness?"

I need someone that doesn't mine telling the fellas that he can't hang with them every night and that he is going to spend some time with his wife. I need someone that doesn't have jealous friends that would take him away from his family because they do not have a wife that would honor them. I need a spouse that would say yes to Jesus, humble himself to God, and treat my son, grandson, and me with respect.

God allowed me to be broken to teach me a lesson. I had sinned against God and I believe that's why I went through so much hell is this last marriage. I didn't represent God well, and I pray that I didn't lead people away from God for my foolish and lustful desires. I refuse to go through another marriage like I have had in the past. I am allowing God to fully heal me so that I can have a marriage that is led according to the word of God and not the lust of my eyes, the lust of my flesh, nor the pride of life.

NINETEEN

My Best Friend Maestro

I AM WAITING on God to send me a spouse. My niece and one of her friends introduced me to Maestro. That's the name that I gave him. He has several talents like: Video Editor, Song Writer, Composer, Music Producer, Singer, and a Musician. His real name is Frederick William Woodfield, but he is known by "**1Bro. Fred.**" I consider him to be my best friend. We really enjoy music, talking about the word of God, and praying together. He's an awesome writer who writes gospel rap songs, and he is taking keyboard lessons. He has so many gospel songs that are going to be released and he is currently writing his book. He makes some nice beats as well. He has a zeal for God and music. He makes me laugh and sometimes even though we are several states away, we watch movies together by video chat. I thank God for him, his daughter, and his dog being a part of my life. We encourage each other in the Lord. I pray that I will see the day whenever he releases his music and book to the world.

TWENTY

The Holy Spirit Comforts Me

I THANK GOD for the Holy Spirit. Today is December 29, 2008. I've had one of the worst panic attacks today than in a long time. I knew that I had to go pick up my son from Durham, North Carolina from his father's house. I had an anxiety attack while I was driving from the time that I had left Wilson, NC up to the time that I had reached Bailey, North Carolina. My mind and body felt like I couldn't make it. I felt a blank as if somebody was having problems with a drop in his sugar level. My heart began beating so fast. It was pounding and I was beginning to sweat.

I know that deliverance came for me when I starting praying in the Holy Spirit. I asked God to help me. I started praying in the Holy Spirit. I do not know what I was praying, but I do know without a shadow of a doubt that whatever spirit was trying to attack my mind and my body, Jesus came to my rescue. I've had to pray like this so many times in order to help me focus on how to drive.

I have often thought that people would think that I was crazy by me talking to myself. It didn't matter. I wanted deliverance. I always get the deliverance that I need whenever I go into the spiritual realm and talk to Jesus. I do not call on any other spirit other than the Holy

Spirit. **St. John 14:26 "Howbeit when he, the Spirit of truth is come, he will guide you into all truth: for he shall not speak of himself; but whatsoever he shall hear, that shall he speak: and he will shew you things to come. He shall glorify me: for he shall receive of mine, and shall shew it unto you." Acts 1:8 "But ye shall receive power, after that the Holy Ghost is come upon you: and ye shall be witnesses unto me both in Jerusalem, and in all Judaea, and in Samaria, and unto the uttermost part of the earth."**

The Holy Spirit, also known as the Holy Ghost, was sent to the saints to do ministry with after Jesus went back to the Father. He brings all things back to our remembrance. The Holy Ghost comforts us, helps us to be a witness, and He also speaks to us and give us insight on the future at times.

Something happens whenever I pray in the Holy Spirit. Peace comes over me. I can feel the presence of God. According to the word of God, mysteries are spoken whenever one prays in the Holy Ghost. **I Corinthians 14:2 "For he that speaketh in an unknown tongue speaketh not unto men, but unto God; for no man understan-deth him; hobeit in the spirit he speaketh mysteries."**

TWENTY-ONE

Encouragement to Others

I WANT TO say to all of mankind that God loves you. God hates sin, but He loves the saints, back sliders, and sinners. In John 3:16, Jesus came that we all might have life and have it more abundantly. **John 3:16 "For God so loved the world, that he gave his only begotten Son, that whosoever believeth in him should not perish, but have everlasting life." Romans 10:9–10** is just the beginning for our salvation. **Romans 10:9–10 "That if thou shalt confess with thy mouth the Lord Jesus, and shalt believe in thine heart that God hath raised him from the dead, thou shalt be saved. For with the heart man believeth unto righteousness; and with the mouth confession is made unto righteousness."**

I hope that those that are alive will accept Jesus Christ before it is too late. None of us are perfect. We all make mistakes. We need to accept Jesus Christ and then allow Him to help us to put down all the things in our lives that are not pleasing to Him. I thank God for whoever came up with this saying about "Let's catch the fish and then we can clean them." God wants all of us to be saved, and then if we will allow Him to, He will clean us up. We don't have the power to save ourselves, but the Holy Spirit has that power to save us and keep us in perfect peace whenever we keep our minds stayed on Jesus. We are fishers of men as Christians. I want every individual to know that he or she is important, and to never give up on his or her dreams. God is the only one that can make our dreams come true and cause us to walk in our destiny.

The times in which we live in today, a lot of people are very selfish. Sometimes people are walking all on top of others just to get his or her needs met. Please be aware of the Devil and his different devices that he uses to hurt people. **John 10:10 "The thief cometh not, but for to steal, and to kill, and to destroy: I am come that they might have life, and that they might have it more abundantly."** Look at the things that I have gone through in life whenever I have been so disobedient to good authority and disobedient unto God. Now, I choose that life. I can't take another fail nothing. I have to be on the winning team. The winning team is only through Christ Jesus. He said that it is finished. We that be in Christ already win. Jesus Christ gave us the victory through His birth, death, and resurrection.

Every decision that I make in life doesn't only affect me. It affects everyone and everything that I am connected to. I am so careful to watch who and what activity comes into my space because I want to stay on the winning team. That winning team is the Light in the Midst of Darkness! I choose life today.

BIBLIOGRAPHY

The Bible. (Denotes King James Version)

Lofton, Johnie Ray. Telephone interview. 28 Dec. 2008.

www.ingramcontent.com/pod-product-compliance
Lightning Source LLC
Chambersburg PA
CBHW021003150626
46549CB00012BA/1051